CENTERING

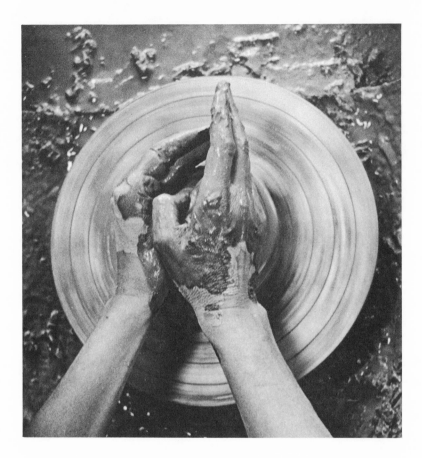

CENTERING

in Pottery, Poetry, and

the Person

By

MARY CAROLINE RICHARDS

Second Edition

Wesleyan University Press, Middletown, Connecticut

LIBRARY OF CONGRESS CATALOGING-IN-PUBLICATION DATA
Richards, Mary Caroline.
    Centering in pottery, poetry, and the person / by Mary Caroline
Richards. — 2nd ed.
        p.   cm.
    ISBN 0-8195-5190-2   ISBN 0-8195-6200-9 (pbk.)
    1. Self-actualization (Psychology)   2. Self-realization.
I. Title.
BF637.S4R52   1989
158'.1—dc19   88-38316
                                                       CIP

Manufactured in the United States of America
First Edition, 1964
Second Edition, 1989
Wesleyan Paperback, 1989

93   92   91   90   5   4   3   2

"For the good man to realize
that it is better to be whole
than to be good
is to enter on a strait and
narrow path compared to which
his previous rectitude was
flowery licence."

—*John Middleton Murry*

"Dann man gerade nur denkt, wenn, das worüber man denkt,
man gar nicht ausdenken kann."
(*Then only are we really thinking when the subject on
which we are thinking cannot be thought out.*)

—*Goethe*

Foreword to the Second Edition

"Ideas do not belong to people. Ideas live in the world as we do. We discover certain ideas at certain times." So writes M. C. Richards in *Centering: In Pottery, Poetry, and the Person* (p. 28), a book that has touched and influenced tens of thousands of people in the twenty-five years of its "living in the world as we do." I consider this book one of the great works of American philosophy: it is so cosmological, so feminist (without once using that term), so original, so full of wisdom, so post-Cartesian, so non-dualistic, so moral, and so fully a part of the mystical tradition of the West that one wonders from what source it arrived in our world. Was it a virgin birth? Whatever its source, I am certain this book will endure. For it is truthful from an ancient, pre-patriarchal, source of truth. It is truthful from the source of our bodies, our bodying forth, our clay-being and our movement being. As long as we are clay and as long as we can move and make move we shall learn from this book.

Who is this author who challenges us to imagine "inventing yellow" or "a cherry curve" (p. 70)? She tells us that she is one who "listen[s] to what is not audible" and tries "to say what is not speakable" (p. 146). Should we allow her to play with us this way? Is she mocking us all, or just our condition? Or is she living the ancient mystical truth of paradox and humor and letting go? Is she urging us to develop what Meister Eckhart calls "unselfconsciousness"? Clearly the author is a mystic who is in love with the ineffable—as all mystics are. She appears to have more courage than many mystics do, however, judging from the vast scope of this book.

We all have our motives for continuing to read this book even though it frustrates and challenges and disturbs and destroys. Like the prophets of old, the author "roots up and destroys" as well as "builds and plants" (Jeremiah 1 : 10). This is a prophetic and mystical book. Such books are dangerous. They are the kind dictators burn, churches tend to ignore, and consumer cultures leave on the shelf. For they have the power to awaken, to stir, to disturb, and to transform. I have heard many stories these past twelve years (since I personally came upon this work) from people whose lives were as deeply affected as my own by this work. I shall merely tell my story.

The first time I read this book I was in the process of designing a master's program in spirituality. I had traveled the country examining all the spirituality programs then in existence and had written a report in which I summarized my findings: all were lacking in their treatment of the role of art, justice, feminism, and body, and all were lacking practical tools for drawing the mystic out of persons. I concluded that a new model was necessary to truly educate (i.e., to evoke growth) in spirituality. The heart of this model must be what I called, based on Claudio Naranjo's work, "extrovert meditation" or "art as meditation." I eventually began such a program and have been heavily involved in it for the past twelve years. In the initial planning stages I had doubts: Who am I to throw out two hundred years of Descartes's educational philosophy? What makes you so sure art is the missing ingredient in education? If art is so central to mysticism then why haven't more persons who were mystics told us so? If you say everyone is an artist aren't you destroying the vocation of the especially gifted one? Then I read M. C. Richards's *Centering*. I realized I was not alone. If I was a crazy educator, I was in good company! If I was a slayer of the artist in my effort to draw the artist out of everyone, at least I had a willing accomplice.

At that time I wrote an article, "The Case for Extrovert Meditation," that has become something of a staple piece for anyone attending our Institute in Culture and Creation Spirituality. In that article I interact with M. C. Richards and Claudio Naranjo. *Centering* has become a kind of Bible for the nine thousand students who have studied with us over the years. Meeting M. C. Richards, viewing an exhibit of her clay work, observing the effect she has on students when I listen to her lecture, working with her in summer programs in Philadelphia and in Ireland have been among the highpoints of my life. The first time we worked together, she celebrated her seventieth birthday. To do the occasion justice, she went out that day and got her ears pierced! After a workshop in Dublin, we took a day to travel the craggy, ocean coastline of Galway together. M. C. pulled out a small set of paints, and we stopped and sat on rocks to paint together the colors within and without. She kept shouting one refrain to me: "more color, more color!" From that trip on, I have found it increasingly necessary to work with paints. And lots of color!

M. C. Richards is dangerous. She practices what she preaches. She has written a truly subversive book. No one who is unaccustomed to danger or unprepared to deal with it should read this book. For, like all great teachers of mysticism, M. C. Richards does not coddle us or hide the truth from us. She warns us, for example, that there are "deeper meanings than those of private sensation" (p. 4). I would propose this as one of the most important antisentimental statements in American philosophy. Instead of succumbing to the sentimentalism that so pervades our culture, she invites us to journey deeper. Instead of hiding the truth from us, she elicits it from within us—as Jesus did by speaking in parables. To do what she does can endanger one's lifestyle, one's citizenship, one's way of seeing the world, one's level of comfort.

If, after all these fair warnings, you still want to read on, I shall name some of the disturbing themes that M. C. introduces to our philosophies of living and educating in the latter part of the twentieth century. The most amazing accomplishment of this book is the author's integration of a living cosmology and a practical mysticism. M. C. reconnects the cosmos with the person through the spiritual discipline of centering. This is no modest accomplishment for the disease of anthropocentrism is, in my opinion, what most haunts the one-sided and therefore violent psyche of the West.

Cosmology is the marriage of science (the elders telling us the story of our origins) to mysticism (the response of awe to our origins) and to art (the expression of the awesome story of our being here). M. C. Richards critiques how bereft we have been of a living cosmology in the West when she says:

> The ordinary so-called science and so-called religion of our day, in the civilization of the West, tend to conduct a cold war of their own. They attempt to co-exist and to divide the world between them. There is palpable disunion. This split obstructs the poetic consciousness; it is a characteristic malady of our society. . . . The inner soul withdraws, goes underground, splits off from the part that keeps walking around. Vitality ebbs. Psychic disturbance is acute. Suicide may be attempted (p. 60).

The author offers her own insights on what a healthy cosmology can do for us. "[L]ove is fostered by a capacity to experience cosmos," she writes unashamedly (p. 107). And when we are cosmological we are *all* poets, for one is a poet who "feels and tells through his being the whole story" (p. 67). In a radically nonanthropocentric observation she celebrates the mystical union of "the intelligence of the clay, my intelligence, the intelligence of the tools, the intelligence of the fire" that come together on the potter's wheel (p. 15). Those who can celebrate as unself-consciously as M. C. does the "intelligence" of clay, of tools, of fire, and of themselves have already slain the dragon anthropocentrism.

M. C. does not hesitate to draw moral lessons from her cosmology. She tells us that "the laws of physics are the laws of our nature, or else they are not laws at all" (p. 37). She teaches us that "the world is always bigger than one's own focus" (p. 21). How cosmic she is, always cosmic! She demands that we open up to the universe. She tells us where wisdom comes from by teaching us that morality emerges from "religion, science, and art operating out of the same nucleus" (p. 142). It is little wonder that her book begins with an invitation to "seek to bring universe into personal wholeness" (p. 3). How regrettable it is that religion, science, and art have been at odds, gone their own specialized ways, these past few centuries thus rendering us without moral imagination or power.

Because M. C. is so committed to a cosmology, she offers morality without moralizing. Morality for her is to "commit ourselves to participation" (p. 92), and from this participation derives the development of moral imagination. Another way of naming this capacity for moral participation is compassion: "the ability to picture the sufferings of others, to identify. In one's citizenship, or the art of politics, it is part of one's skill to imagine other ways of living than one's own" (p. 115). Compassion is itself an alternative "mode of perception." It is the ultimate act of centering, of bringing together the known energies of the universe. I am reminded of Jesus who teaches in his Sermon on the Mount: "Be you compassionate as your Creator in heaven is compassionate" (Luke 7:36), and of Meister Eckhart who says: "The first outburst of everything God does is always compassion."[1] M. C. Richards, in inviting us to compassion, is inviting us to our origins . . . and beyond, to the alpha and omega of our existence. And she teaches us the way.

The way is one of perception. Awakening our perceptions; cleansing our perceptions; celebrating our perceptions; reverencing our perceptions. The artist in us must lead the way into this spiritual voyaging—for the artist in us *perceives*. "We want our minds to be clear—not so we can think clearly, but so we can be open in our perceptions" (p. 37). Notice what M. C. does so subtly here: she rejects Descartes's (and patriarchy's!) philosophy that "I think therefore I am" with a radical invitation to perceive. "We perceive, therefore we are." Or better, "We are open in our perceptions and therefore we exist." The point is that we are not responsible for our existence; existence already floods us—but we can resist the flood, clog our minds, freeze our hearts, imprison our bodies, defend our senses *against* it. Nature itself is already giving us existence, buttressing it, overwhelming us with its awe and wonder.

All we need do to begin is to open up and perceive. As M. C. puts it, "it is not a concept that I wish to convey. It is, rather, an experience of nature which I wish to summon into consciousness. It comes in like a light, clearing the mind. . . . It is not a matter of 'adding to' but of 'developing,' of 'evolving'" (p. 37). Light is a given; we are the receivers *and*, by imagination, rebirthers of the light. But first we must perceive this. M. C. cites Henry James who said that a writer is a person upon whom nothing is lost—but she improves on James when she adds, "Well, anyone should be: a person upon whom nothing is lost!" (p. 106). M. C. celebrates our powers of perception. She sees the true capacity of these powers to "take in more and more of the universe" (p. 106) as a counterpoint to merely developing our capacities to taste. "I am not primarily concerned with what we like. I am concerned with our power to grasp, to comprehend, to penetrate, and to embrace" (p. 106). Craft means power. Power is what spirituality is about—not taste but the power to perceive, to receive, to create, and to transform.

In developing this rich and essential theme M. C. Richards is elaborating on the spiritual path of the *via positiva*. She points out that we have to let things be if we are to ground ourselves in the gift that simply being here entails. She writes:

> Acceptance is part of love. It is devotion to the whole. When the doctrine of acceptance speaks of doing away with the categories of good and evil, it is not in order to turn everything into good, nor to turn everything into nothing. Rather it is to prepare a meeting between man and phenomena at a level free of category, of evaluation. This is a preparation for the acceptance of the 'is-ness' of each thing (p. 139).

Here again, M. C. speaks in the mystical tradition of giants like Meister Eckhart who says that "is-ness is God." But she does so at the practical level of preparing us to experience is-ness. Her doctrine of acceptance becomes the starting point for the mystical journey, a further deepening of the *via positiva*, the way of opening up to the light, the Cosmic Christ, the Cosmic Wisdom, that each being bears within its own divine, "I am." As she puts it, "At the center, Christ, Atman, I and It" (p. 138).

But M. C.'s self-styled doctrine of acceptance is not only about accepting the divine light, but also the divine absence, the searing darkness, the infinite estrangement, the plunging emptiness. Her doctrine applies to the *via negativa* of the mystical way as well. She names the experience of entering the dark as well as any mystic ever has:

> I am brought to a crisis because I am committed to acceptance and to the suffering it entails. I have to accept the separation in order to keep contact with the shape experience is taking. I must keep my clay centered. . . . In order to accept mistrust, I have to experience *that* and live into *its* meaning. Acceptance is not a nod of civility, nor is it approval. It is something more like ingestion, a capacity to experience the reality of another not as if it were one's own but indeed as another's, a capacity for self-surrender . . . not of the will but of the perception (p. 140).

Armed with this dance of perception (*via positiva*) and acceptance (*via negativa*), M. C. can rightly claim that "perception itself yields moral insight." There is no morality without art; no conscience without cosmos; no act of participation, i.e., morality and compassion, without imagination. All of which explains the moral stupor in which Western civilization—bereft of cosmology, mysticism, and art—finds itself in today. Compassion, after all is said and done, "is a mode of perception" (p. 115). No wonder the exercising of our perception is a requisite for the moral and spiritual initiative that compassion is about. The seed of imagination exists in all of us as children, and, with it, the potential *tree* of compassion. "From the child's capacity to imagine grows as well the adult's capacity for compassion: the ability to picture the sufferings of others, to identify" (p. 115). But perhaps we ought not take the child's capacity to imagine too literally, for M. C. may be challenging every adult to recover the child within, who still harbors a seed of imagination destined to flower into a tree. Is this any different from Jesus's teaching that "unless you adults turn and become like this child you shall never enter into the kingdom/queendom of God" (Matthew 18:4)? Like Jesus, M. C. is calling upon people to see with their hearts, to perceive, that "the kingdom/queendom of

God *is* among you" (Luke 17 : 21). The divine kingdom/queendom is creation itself, the cosmos alive and resplendent with divine presence. If only we had ears to hear and eyes to see and hearts to listen. But we do! That is M. C.'s teaching.

M. C. Richards is old-fashioned in her morality. She believes in justice. "Compassion means justice," wrote Meister Eckhart six hundred years ago.[2] M. C. concurs. A synonym for justice is "homeostasis" and M. C. sees this as "the body's natural centering process, a tendency that is always operative within it." She sees homeostasis as a universal law, that "anything left to itself will tend to equilibrium." And she sees the centering process that the potter or dancer undergoes as the act of righting things, of making justice happen. "As a dancer shifts his position he keeps his balance. He does this by taking his center with him, he shifts his center of gravity, re-establishing his equilibrium in the very instant that he has leapt. Otherwise he will fall and hurt himself" (p. 38). We are extended such an invitation here—to take our center with us. Spirituality is radically portable. We are troubadours after all, a traveling troupe of center-makers, overcoming the fall, perceiving the laws of gravity, leaping but re-establishing justice and equilibrium in the process. There can be no morality and no spirituality without the artist showing us the way. It is a leap—but a balanced leap—that M. C. makes between justice and perception when she says: "How can we not see what our eyes behold? As our perceptions become more and more coordinated, we grow in justice" (p. 78). Is this why art and the ways of enlarging our perceptions, the spiritual discipline of art as meditation, has been such a rare commodity during a time of injustice? To re-educate ourselves in art is to re-educate ourselves in justice.

How dangerous art can be! Here the *via creativa*—our works of imagination—and the *via transformativa*—our struggle for social justice, healing, transformation, and compassion—come together. All four paths of the mystical/prophetic journey are named by M. C. Richards, and named in practice as well as in theory. The practice is centering. Each of the paths is a kind of centering—a centering on the light and awe of the gratuitous cosmos (path one); a centering on the darkness, the pain, the separations that break into our celebration of is-ness (path two); a centering on that seed of imagination lurking in the darkness and underneath the soil and a surrender to our native capacities for giving birth (path three); and a centering on the imbalance that injustice causes in society and in the person—and bringing moral imagination to bear on that lack of equilibrium (path four). When I use the term "creation-*centered* spirituality" to name this ancient mystical tradition of creativity and compassion, I now know more of what is behind the term "centered," thanks to M. C.'s work:

> As you go out, you come in, you always come into center, bring the clay into center; you press down, squeeze up, press one hand into the other, bringing your material into center. . . . We bring our self into a centering function, which brings it into union with all other elements. This is love. . . . Then the miracle happens: When on center, the self *feels* different: one feels *warm, on rayonne*, in touch, the power of life a substance like an air in which one lives and has one's being with all other things, drinking it in and giving it off, at the same time quiet and at rest within it" (p. 56).

M. C. not only challenges the reader's lack of moral and spiritual sensibilities that derive from the lack of cosmology in our culture, but she also dares to challenge the artist. The artist, no less than the scientist or the religious believer, has been deeply wounded by a culture lacking in cosmology. She confesses on the opening page that it was artists "dry for meaning in their efforts" (p. 3) who urged her to articulate the content of this book. She laments the price the artist is so often forced to pay in our culture—we are all tempted to "abandon poetry for power" (p. 59). This poetry we are so easily tempted to abandon is our "Spiritual Discipline," an "absolute and primal encounter to which we must devotedly surrender." Poetry stretches our feelings and perceptions, our intuitions and "our sense of world as entity" (p. 64f.). In other words, poetry is a centering discipline, a discipline of prayer, a way of developing the mystic within by connecting to all without. Meister Eckhart teaches that "the truth cannot come from outside in but must come from inside out and pass through an inner form."[3] This "passing through an inner form" is the demand that poetry makes on us. The potter's wheel makes the same demand: the demand to center. It is the taking in and the giving out. And what we center is nothing less than the entire universe in which we live, move, and have our being.

"Centering the clay on the potter's wheel and then using it all to make whatever shape one makes; hearing the poem in the exactitude of its words and syllables and lines and in the economy of its total fusion—these are the same story. To bring universe into personal wholeness . . ." (p. 65). Poetry is a "commitment to the Living Air: a faithfulness to breath, to Speech, to Logos" (p. 66). It is the entrance of the cosmic story into the universe.

M. C. warns the artist that art can become merely a "trade" if the artist too is not bent on a spiritual journey and has lost the sense of art as a "bridge between the visible and invisible worlds." Art serves. "Here the importance of centering seems emphatic." The artist is in touch with "the joyful breathing at our source" (p. 94f.). Art serves joy; art serves justice and compassion; art serves the poor, the oppressed, the victims of misbegotten power; art serves mysticism, a "return to our source"; art serves a living cosmology. Art is always bodily. There lies its affront to a cartesian educational ideology and to a patriarchal satisfaction with cognitive knowledge alone, with truth in the head that never penetrates heart or body and therefore fails to heal the body politic. *Centering* is a bodily book, an incarnational work. Born of M. C.'s bodily work on the potter's wheel with the earthy substance that clay and body are. This book renders impossible the unconsciousness of the body. It begs for the reunion of body, mind, and spirit. It is sensual, sexual, trusting, and full of surprises—as all body-spirit energy is. "Wisdom is not the product of mental effort" but a "state of the total being," M. C. warns us, "It is in our bodies that redemption takes place. It is the physicality of the crafts that pleases me: I learn through my hands and my eyes and my skin what I could never learn through my brain" (p. 15). The hand and the clay speak to each other in a fecund dialogue that "is spoken not by the tongue and lips but by the whole body, by the whole person, speaking and listening" (p. 9). What riches art can offer in regaining our sense of the holy erotic, of the pansexual experience of the union of all things; of the sexual archetypes of marriage and union that die when they are overly literalized. What the crafts allow persons to do is "to bring into our bodies the imagination and the will." A primal and personal and material dialogue ensues between "our dreams and the forces of nature" (p. 27). Being an artist is a physical act, a physical discipline, an athletic act, and therefore the root meaning of "asceticism."

I know this even as a writer where hours at a typewriter and with back bent over books can take their toll of sweat and pain. M. C. reports that "the potter has to prepare his body as he does that of the clay." In the process one can learn that "sexuality is a sacrament of the yielding of one center to another" (p. 35). Love-making is another act of pottery, poetry, and centering, and every act of pottery, poetry, and centering is an act of love-making when a living cosmology is the matrix of our work and being.

The artist is a birther of form and form means "bodying forth." All art is a "bodying forth. The bodying forth of the living vessel in the shapes of clay" (p. 39). It is through the body that we experience the most elemental experiences of relatedness, for we live in a world of relationship. We already are related by the demands and truths of our bodies, for "the air we breathe one moment will be breathed by someone else the next and has been breathed by someone else before" (p. 39). We don't have to strive for relationship—relationship already is. It is a grace and not a work. The body absorbs not only the shared air and light of our existence, but also the pollutants, physical and moral, in which we swim together. Prejudice, for example, and our efforts to bully others, are absorbed into our organisms. "This is why it is so important to work curatively through the body as well as through attitudes" (p. 124). The body knows about union because orgasm incorporates the struggle and the stress, the differences and the impulses to union, perception, feeling, and pulse (p. 140).

These are but a few of the many and lasting contributions that this book makes to a healthy philosophy, one that is truly a "love of wisdom" and not a complaint about life or a cynical statement of regret at being born. Nothing I can write could possibly substitute for the actual reading or studying of this amazing and prophetic work. I have been stunned and indeed humbled in my re-reading of this book by the prophetic truths contained in it twenty-five years ago. It is good to know that in our throw-away culture, some things do indeed endure.

The author names her own search (and that of this book) when she discusses education: "It is always the prime question: Where is the moral source? How are the laws to be learned in the human will? How may intellect and sanctity marry? Where does one look for the teaching; and once found, how does one use it?" (p. 130). Where should we look for the teaching? We cannot do better than to look—still another time—at this book. In it there is wisdom that the author herself most likely did not know was pulsing through her as she wrote. "There is wisdom in all creative works," Hildegard of Bingen wrote eight centuries ago. The book *Centering* proves her correct.

Matthew Fox
Oakland, California
September, 1988

NOTES

1. Matthew Fox, *Breakthrough: Meister Eckhart's Creation Spirituality in New Translation* (Garden City, New York: Doubleday Image, 1980), p. 441.
2. Ibid, p. 429.
3. Ibid, p. 399.

Introduction to the Second Edition

Centering is a verb. It is an ongoing process, and here it is, twenty-five years after its first publication, reaffirmed as a book. Twenty-five years, and it has never gone out of print, which indicates the seminal quality of its imagery.

I have said that Centering as an archetype comes through the potter's wheel and the spinning clay taking shape. But archetypes are Beings of special subtlety and paradox. So Centering is not a model, but a way of balancing, a spiritual resource in times of conflict, an imagination. It seems in certain lights to be an alchemical vessel, a retort, which bears an integration of purposes, an integration of levels of consciousness. It can be called to, like a divine ear.

If I were to write the book now, there are two things I would change and one addition I would make. The two elements have evolved in the years between the first writing and now. They are actually connected with our collective consciousness as were the insights of the original.

I would not use the masculine pronoun to designate persons of both sexes. I would not write "man" when I mean "person" or "human being." I would not write, as I did in the original introduction, "Man may be born into the world, a whole man." This would be changed even as our consciousness has changed, has become more discriminating, more subtle, more conscientious: "We may be born into the world as whole persons. We are all women-folk, male or female, featured toward this birth. We are all Mary, virgin and undelivered, to whom the announcement has been made, in whom the infant grows."

Simply, we have outgrown the masculine pronoun as the referent for both sexes. "The changing, changeful person, mobile and intact, finding his way on." Couldn't it be generally agreed to realign the genders, to "changing, changeful persons, finding our way on," or "their way on"? We English majors were fine-tuned to the "one . . . he" syndrome. We did not challenge the assumptions behind the grammar (the politics of language). We learned the rules and practiced them quite unconsciously, docile until meaning began to awaken in us and we began to hear what we were saying. A strong and turbulent time, filled with the juice and joy of our evolving awareness. No blame. For we are well aware of the passionate justification given for continuing in the "man" tradition, especially as it translates from the German generic *Mensch*. And there must surely develop a better solution than the "he/she" or "s/he." This is part of our new work: to find the new forms that will be needed as our minds change . . . as our perceptions widen.

As our minds change . . . metanoia . . . what are the arts of transformation?

The second change I would make is to add to the content a more adequate treatment of antipathy and the Centering process in relation to it. Centering, I say, is the discipline of bringing in (i.e., of sympathy or empathy) rather than of leaving out. Of saying "Yes, Yes" to what we behold. To what is holy *and* to what is unbearable. But my experience tells me now that there is an important crucial stage of saying Yes to a No. For resistance also must be embraced. Not only accepting resistance but practicing it.

The metabolism goes something like this perhaps: We become ill. We injest the illness, say Yes to it. Trust it, listen to what it is telling us. But if we continue in this surrender, we may indeed be overtaken by weakness. A moment in my own biography came when I lifted my hand weakly and admitted, "I have no resistance." I heard myself say the words, and a new impulse faintly beat in my breast. No *resistance* . . . I was a patsy for any wandering virus. I began to feel a kind of feeble indignation. My own interpretation of Centering, it now seems to me, had grown one-sided. It would be the severest discipline for me to integrate the No, to reject, to judge. What was to become of love then, how about loving the enemy and doing good to those who revile us? I "love" the tiger, but I do not put my head in its mouth. What a riddle it is. It was ten years after the publication of *Centering* that I had this conscious breakthrough. I have been a faithful student of the lessons of the potter's wheel. (There's that to be said for me!)

The hardest and most rewarding lesson has been to learn to experience antipathy objectively, with warmth. For antipathy follows a gesture of separating, and the goal, which is to be both separate and connected, requires that one move inwardly in opposite directions. Toward self-definition and toward community. Toward ethical individualism and toward social justice. It is this fusing of the opposites that Centering enables. It is a powerful image that we are given by the potter's art: to "open" the ball of clay as it turns on the wheel, and to alter its destiny as it leaves the commonly rounded ball and develops toward the specifically shaped bowl. This it does between my fingers, which hold the wall of the bowl inside/outside simultaneously. The clay is given and the roundness is given, but the individual shape is one's own creative doing.

The theme of integrating the opposites develops in my work from book to book, the seed having been sown in *Centering*. Another archetypal development comes in the geometric form of the lemniscate (moebus strip), which is the ground of my second book *The Crossing Point*. The crossing point is the name given to the layer of cells out of which the root and the shoot of a plant begin to sprout. The plant grows in opposite directions simultaneously, down into the earth and up into the light and air. The forms of the plant change accordingly. Think of the carrot, for example. All orange and dense and pointed, it digs deep into the soil. And all filigree lace of green foliage above ground, it opens to the sun. The lemniscate is a figure eight as a plane, a ribbon (L. *lemnis*). Its genius is to constitute a continuous form turning now inward and now outward. Follow the upper loop of the eight with your finger outside and go through the crossing point and you will find that your finger is on the inside of the bottom loop and so on. A continuum of opposites. And so, the lesson goes, we may think of the genius of the human being, earth oriented by gravity, with feet on the ground, and in consciousness a weightless being whose head is full of dreams and visions. We do not have to decide which way we will be, practical or visionary, for we are both. And that is our genius.

And now for the thought I would add. It is a kind of advice to the reader to make sure of understanding how Centering is offered in this book. "Center" and "centered" have come to be fairly widely used. They tend to imply a connection with the navel, with one-pointedness, on the way to bliss, realization, and inner peace. But these are not the goals of the Centering process. For it is a continual engagement with experience, not a withdrawal from it. It begins with pain and ends with paradox. It wrestles with evil and the daimonic as it does with angels and repentance. It is an activity of consciousness, not a stage of spiritual achievement. So some readers may assume they already know what Centering is and then translate the imagery of the book into what they already think. This is a very common kind of projection we human beings practice—not really listening anew.

It must be admitted that the experience of Centering is especially ambiguous. For the image of the center appears pivotally in various philosophies and religious practices. Paul Reps, in *Zen Flesh, Zen Bones*, finds it to have been spiritually alive 4000 years ago. It is part of the language of the Quakers also, to speak of a centered meeting, of "centering down," which leads to a focus of attention, of inner listening to the inner voice. The Centering I have learned about from the potter's practice is in some ways the exact opposite of this. For in centering the clay on the potter's wheel, one centers down, yes, and then one immediately centers up! Down and up, wide and narrow, letting focus bear within it an expanded consciousness and letting a widened awareness (empathetic) have the commitment to detail of a focused attention. Not "either . . . or," but "both . . . and." You can perhaps feel the inner movement of a Centering consciousness that plays dynamically in the tides of inner and outer, self and other, in an instinctive hope toward wholeness. Carl Gustav Jung speaks of our psyche's transcendent function. Perhaps Centering has something of that color.

I have found that Centering, like clay, wears well! It bears the future within it. For it contains a space for ongoing development and differentiation. In other words, it proves to be an open image, a vessel, holding a content that is life itself. In the quarter century since I was asked by Wesleyan University Press to write this book (as an offering in their new department of interdisciplinary works), I have allowed the basic imagery to move and to attract a broader vocabulary until what has been inherent from the beginning has become an explicit study of "wholeness." Later works, *Toward Wholeness: Rudolf Steiner Education in America* and *The Public School and the Education of the Whole Person*, attest to this.

Like *Centering*, these works were invited or "commissioned" by a publisher. This fact indicates, I think, that there is something more working here than personal taste. There is an actual movement in the collective psyche of our society that mirrors itself in the appearance of certain concerns—synchronistically, you might say; that is, all at the same time in different places! It was particularly exciting to me to come upon David Bohm's *Wholeness and the Implicate Order* in 1980 just at the moment when my own work bearing "wholeness" in its title appeared. Bohm is a theoretical physicist at the University of London, and he came to his picture of reality through the disciplines of science. I came to mine through God knows what diverse intersections of the arts and humanities. Bohm and I were graduate students at the University of California at Berkeley at the same time, though we never met at that time. Forty years later, having gone by very different ways, we receive from archetypal consciousness the same message. An evolution of consciousness, yes. Others also had been listening: Gregory Bateson in *Mind and Nature, a Necessary Unity* and Fritjof Capra in *The Tao of Physics* and *The Turning Point*. Likewise Ilya Prigogine, the Belgian biochemist who won the Nobel prize for his discoveries about entropy and its relation (i.e., the relation of dissipative structures) to creativity. Pralaya, chaos, the space between, these are being assimilated as part of a wholeness, not a threat or an exception.

We find on so many fronts now, political and artistic as well as religious and economic, an imaginative thrust that goes not toward competitive violence and adversary motifs, but toward new social forms. Imagination is more and more recognized as a form of cognition, and inspiration and intuition are coming on fast. Owen Barfield's work in the history of consciousness and of language has contributed new ground for new insights. It is particularly moving to find the physicist Bohm saying that reality cannot be described statistically—that it lends itself much more to the way of understanding one might have of the arts, of poetry and dance for example, though it is in *music* that he finds the leading paradigm. This is not aesthetics but morphology.

In the light of these developments, we can extend our image beyond pottery and speak of "artistic mind." That is, mind that makes connections between things ordinarily thought to be different. This, Aristotle long ago declared, is the highest human capacity; it is the capacity for metaphor. It is what makes poets of us all. Ah, but as soon as one begins to use phrases like "artistic mind," all the other claimants to our connecting capacities rush forward protesting an artistic conceit and takeover. How about "religious mind"? For "religion" also, like "art," bears within its history as a word the very shape of reconnecting, of joining. And "scientific mind," how about that, the darling of our cultural epoch? For in the word "science"—"knowing"—too, we hear the ancient coupling of opposites, of man and wife—for through cognition one unites with another. In biblical language, the husband knows his wife, that is, unites with her in the flesh.

xxi

To know is to unite with in the flesh. Isn't this an inspiring reminder of Plato's "to know the good is to do the good"—though by now we are very able to know and not do. For us now the doing has to be a free choice out of our destiny, without pressure. For this is what fires our hearts, is it not? To feel ourselves free to love and to live. Unbullied and unbullying. Unhaunted by a conscience made guilty by social pressures and expectations. To act from source freely.

This connection between vision and practice, between knowing and creating, is richly portrayed in the experience of the young Oglala Sioux Indian Black Elk, as he tells it to John Neihardt in the book *Black Elk Speaks*. Black Elk has had a tremendous dream (a *mysterium tremendum*) as a child during an illness. In the dream he goes to the Grandfathers of the Flaming Rainbow Teepee and they give him gifts from each direction: the cup from the Grandfather of the West to catch the rainwater from thunderstorms; the peace pipe from the Grandfather of the North; the flowering branch from the Grandfather of the South; the four-petaled herb of healing from the East. The dream is filled with thronging horses and great birds as well. The boy does not speak of his dream to his family or friends. When he is seventeen he begins to suffer anxiety attacks upon the approach of storms from the West. Finally, in extreme agitation, he goes to a medicine man for help. The medicine man tells him, "For a person who has a vision, you do not get the power of your vision until you perform it on earth for the people to see." Aha! Black Elk then creates dances for his tribe to express the mysteries and gifts of the vision. For it was a vision of wholeness, of the hoop of the world and the tribes all dancing in peace within it. *You do not get the power of your vision until you perform it on earth for the people to see!*

Is it some of this leaven that has brought me at the present time to live in a working community with mentally handicapped adults based on biodynamic agriculture: farming and gardening? To practice what I preach. To move in the direction of that from which one feels most separated as well as confirming one's stance in what has already evolved. Here I have a pottery studio where I can be private—and a larger space where I offer open studio sessions for people in our village. I am a member of a household, sharing in cooking and parenting. In the gardening season, I am a fine-tuned weeder in the herb garden. And I give a course in our agricultural training program, which I call (it makes me merry) "The Renewal of Art through Agriculture." To clay I add writing and coloring, and the context that supports our efforts is landscape itself and its metaphors—the world of formative forces that shape us inwardly and outwardly, from bones to scarecrows, from budthrusts to fallen rock—a texture of polarities. Biodynamic agriculture goes a step beyond organic farming in that it sprays the earth with special substances that strengthen its vital forces. Much of the earth is suffering from burnout, depletion of etheric forces, leeching of essential minerals. And the food we grow likewise may suffer nutritive loss. But this can be rebuilt, can be healed, and many now are serving the earth in a new awareness of the interdependence of its body and our bodies.

To do the work of the earth and to build community are new priorities. The one has a wonderful supportive daily and seasonal rhythm, connected with the stars and planets in a cosmic cycle. The other is like a glowworm lighting up the dark here and there. I have been guided to this life-school by the spirit of Centering, as I learn to live with individuals whom I have not chosen as friends. And to live with people whose supposed "handicaps" challenge our social stereotypes right down the line.

The handicapped have a special role to play in the inspiration of community. They teach us to be concrete, to be particular. They have no gift for abstraction. It is now. It is here. It is this kind of question they ask, "Is yesterday gone yet?" We see ourselves mirrored in their helplessness before onslaughts of feeling or sensory overload. Emotionally we are mostly still in our childhood and adolescence. How much we need to grow toward healing. We will do it together. Soon the "they" will disappear into a larger "we." For we may begin to perceive the sorrows and cruelties of our society as developmental—that is, we are handicapped by our autism (selfish self-absorption) and our hysteria (spaced-out consciousness) and our epilepsy (fits of contraction, hardening, self-abuse, out-of-control horror at our own impotence). By accepting suffering, we may relate more to others, developing compassion. By grace we may come free. And best of all we may find our sense of humor enormously expanded through the warmth of our heart center, that deepset crossing point.

One last testimony to the metabolism of Centering. It is new! It brings us what we don't already know. We have not seen it face to face, but we have had sightings. They have come through language with an alteration in the traditional roles of poetry and prose. I do not think now about which one I am writing in, except when my soul begins to feel as if there is too much light, too much clarity, too much illusion of meaning, of earnestness, too much spirit—and then I dive for cover, for dark, for wet, and come up moistened and renewed, and speaking (or singing) a different tone.

The balloon softens as it lands, and shapes itself to the contours of the earth.

Twenty-five years ago, Centering moved swiftly and unconsciously into image and interpretation. Since then it has grown more conscious, more connected with more themes, more explicit. Its speech seems to me to be, at heart, mantric. To stay in mantric consciousness and to expand one's references is a task. Thus do sacred and secular marry to bear a new person into the world. As that new person, we may find, yes, that yesterday is over, and we do not perpetuate old confusions. We do not cling to the savagery of nationalisms, or the shame we feel for being as we are. We stand on the shore of an ocean and the pure wind blows us fresh and we wake out of an anguish of inner conflict into a deep breath that lets us rise to our feet and in a new levity we dance. It could be said that fidelity to the processes of Centering is a path to full breathing, to a balance willingly at risk.

I have a special friend, Julia Connor, who is a poet and who calls me *O wild and nameless*! It is to the divine ear she is calling. The suffering we undergo when forms are preferred over spontaneous perception is called culture. We are shaped and intimidated by striving. For human beings are wild and nameless, as well as proper and pedigreed. We drink from the streaming breasts of the god beyond knowing and naming and cannot bear the rituals and liturgies that separate us from them.

This book ends with a birth: the inner child finding its way on, both by visible means and by a visionary trueness (as one might speak of trueing up the lines of ordinary sense perception). We age toward youth, toward our growing tip, which lives as the meristem in even the oldest oak.

M. C. Richards
Kimberton Hills, Pennsylvania
March, 1988

Contents

CENTERING

The Arithmetic, the Bush, and the Plan

BECAUSE I am a potter, I take my image, CENTERING, from the potter's craft. A potter brings his clay into center on the potter's wheel, and then he gives it whatever shape he wishes. There are wide correspondences to this process. Such extensions of meaning I want to call attention to. For CENTERING is my theme: how we may seek to bring universe into a personal wholeness, and into act the rich life which moves so mysteriously and decisively in our bodies, manifesting in speech and gesture, materializing as force in the world the unifying energy of our perceptions.

This book began when I accepted an invitation to give an "inspirational" speech to craftsmen, who said they were dry for meaning in their efforts. They asked me because I am teacher and poet as well as potter. They wanted "the contemplations of the poet upon the craft." I decided to share with my hosts certain meanings that had inspired me: stilling my thirst, opening my eyes, freeing my imagination and hearing, strengthening my nerve, inspiriting my limbs. On the basis of the response, Wesleyan University Press asked for a book-length elaboration of the themes I had broached. "We would like to have your spirit between hard covers." Why? Because, they implied, my experience builds bridges between disciplines which are often considered separate if not antagonistic. This press wishes to speak to the need for interdisciplinary participation.

I have written this book out of the feel of a process, and a feel of commitment to it. I speak from and to a diverse fellowship: in the arts and thought and research, poets and

3

craftsmen and students and teachers, homemakers and community members and solitary citizens.

The imagery of centering is archetypal.

To feel the whole in every part:

The Mystery and Action and Being of the whole living organism of oneself and of that Self which all of us together make, and of that earth where we are humanly born, and of that sun-sphere that nourishes us too, and of all that universe that beats its way to us now through millions of trillions of light years, making our future its long past, and making the double-talk of mystics who drown time like a puppy in the flood of something else seem like a handbook to cosmic thinking, home style.

It is my hope to create a mood which will inspire and strengthen a confidence in man and his life earthwise and cosmic. A mood sympathetic to natural processes of forming and transforming. Human beings have many stories to tell, and this is one of them. I sense things that have happened to me as somehow characteristic of the human lot, transcending personality, bearing within them a form which can reveal to my consciousness and to others deeper meanings than those of private sensation. I sense structures everywhere at work, in realms to which sensations lead us but where they change into insight and compassion. The deeper we go into these realms, the more contact we make with another's reality. The sharper the sense of pain and bliss as they interweave through the heartbreak and luck of life, the more the line between self and other may dissolve. It is a physique-soul-alchemy: a transformation of inner and outer. This book is a story of transformation.

Its autobiographical aspect arose as I have said, and is emblematic. I claim that the center holds us all, and as we speak out of it, we speak in a common voice. It is as well my part of a common pledge: for I ask others how they have come to believe as they do. What we profess is spiritual autobiography, whether it be science or myth or religion or politics or art or educational philosophy. What I know about centering makes it impossible for me to pretend that truth is either objective or subjective; the practice of centering casts upon such dualisms another light. I very much hope that a relish for person and personal destiny will be conveyed from my breast to the reader's, that he experience himself in full depth, and experiencing himself so, confirm his capacity to experience his fellow man. There is this path forward, to One Another.

The arithmetic of this book is suggested in the image of person and of mankind as many-membered being.

As I read through what I have written during these past months, I get the impression of a shifting rhythm in the landscape, as from the shaggy crown of a thicket to the formal economy of its skeleton. Certain areas seem to me to want cropping, but there is something in their shape that seems true if not trim, and so I leave them to show themselves.

This book is like a bush; it grows from a single root, many branches, many leaves and twigs, but all the same plant. Many resemblances, as one branch and its leaves look like another, except when you look closely. But there the whole thing is: structure and foliage. And there is a plan, which was gradually disclosed to me as I wrote.

The speech out of which it grew was entitled "Centering as Dialogue" and appears, somewhat expanded, as the first chapter. The direction seemed given: Centering, in pottery, poetry, person (and person on the education hook as well as hanging by his thumbs in that most unique and most ultimate "moral" fire). Also the need to hear it, as in tones of voice, seemed inherent.

In Chapter Two, "Centering as Transformation," the theme is strained more through the mesh of person, but keeping him intact — craftsman, student, teacher, social being, anarchist, all he may be. It pushes as far as I can push, to birth and death, life and death, getting them centered, unseparated (this is where Chapter One had ended); and this still seen through craft, through education as lived life, through art, and so on. Always I try to go toward, not formulation, but organism.

In Chapter Three, I offer "Poetry," my own mainly, as witness to the discipline this book is struggling with, toward.

In Chapter Four, "Pedagogy," I lay out as much of the picture as I have of what the centering impulse can bring to education. By now it is evident that the ingredients of every chapter are constant, the focus shifting.

Finally, "Ordeal by Fire": the image, again, takes shape partly from the potter's craft, this time the firing of his kiln, partly from ur-fire, hell-fire, fire of suffering, fire from which the phoenix rises, fire that attests to the innocence of its victims by leaving them unconsumed, the purifying fire. The final form taken. This time I hit very hard the MORAL question: how do we do it, center in the moral sphere? how do we love our enemies?

5

How do we perform the CRAFT of life, *kraft, potentia? Potentia,* like so many other words, has had its meanings separated out, and has come, in our day, to be both *potency* and *potentiality* — that is to say, both the power present and the power latent, that can but has not yet come into being. In Latin these are the same word. And this is a wisdom. For the potentiality is also a present power with which we must deal and to which we must speak. A condition of generative potency, a possibility in persons and things, not yet visible in force but present in seed. In this chapter I speak about what I call Crisis of Conscience and of how art is a Moral Eye, opening and closing. Here the subject of Centering moves into Moral Evolution, how the center itself, in its initiating power, evolves in its form.

This book has not only a plan but a music. Its form is a demonstration of what I say in it. Themes recur and vary. There are passages of development and recapitulation. I wish to offer its meaning not as rationale but as physical presence in language. Iteration and reiteration like days in a season, and we come to the feel of its weather. It aspires to both prose clarity and poetic clarity, though perhaps not at the same moment. Sudden changes of tone — from refinement to coarseness, from mechanics to rapture — are moods of nature. The inquiry is poetic, in that it attempts to keep to the varying rhythms of the hunt.

It is not my wish, however fierce my tone may seem, it is not at all my wish to program behavior. As a matter of fact, I consider all programs to be illusions. There is never any question in my mind who is in the driver's seat. It is for each of us freely to choose WHOM we shall serve, and find in that obedience our freedom. Paradox is at the center. The dynamic of life and death lies in every instant. On what a tender thread we walk.

Centering is the image I use for the process of balance which will enable us to step along that thread feeling it not as a thread but a sphere. It will, it is hoped, help us to walk through extremes with an incorruptible instinct for wholeness, finding our way continuous, self-completing. This thread can be as limber as breath. It is as tough as a wild grape vine. Continuity, of movement and variation and organic process and appearing and disappearing and fruitfulness and withering and seeding, lives in the image of *the vine,* upon which hangs the long poem which ends this book.

6

I am an odd bird in both academic and craft worlds, perhaps because I am a poet, and thus, by calling, busy with seeing the similarities between things ordinarily thought to be different, busy with feeling the sense of relatedness grow through my limbs like a smoke-tree wafting and fusing its images, busy with the innerness of outerness, eating life in its layers like a magic cake made of silica sounds shapes and temperatures and all the things that appear to be separated stacked together in transparencies of color, and it is perhaps my vocation to swallow it whole. The expanding universe. The resilient appetite. The continuous play. The changing, changeful person, mobile and intact, finding his way on.

This is the main thing. This is what I care about, it is the person. This is the living vessel: person. This is what matters. This is our universe. This is the task, the joy and dolor: to be born as person, to live and love as person, to dwell in the World as in a Person. The living spirit, the moving form, the living word, life-death, art-life, *corpus,* body, being, all, persons. Truly life is absent in the moment when person is eliminated. This is the urgency of my speech — for this occasion and all human occasions — to bring man into man's consciousness. It is the presence of person that compels my energy. For life — I am sure of this — is not transforming energy, but transforming person. Energy is the means. Being is not *what* but *whom.* It is Presence in whom and before whom we show ourselves. Let us ride our lives like natural beasts, like tempests, like the bounce of a ball or the slightest ambiguous hovering of ash, the drift of scent: let us stick to those currents that can carry us, membering them with our souls. Our world personifies us, we know ourselves by it. Let us then speak to each other in our most intimate concern. I have been encouraged to speak so in this book.

Man may be born into the world, a whole man. We are all women-folk, male or female, featured toward this birth. We are all Mary, virgin and undelivered, to whom the announcement has been made, in whom the infant grows.

As I read the newspapers, talk with friends, teach my classes, I can tell the hunt is on. I can hear everyone questing, for manhood; I can hear the belling and baying, the hoofs, the trembling ground. Everywhere the mystery of man is being searched out. Where? Where am I? Who?

What I want to say to you here about our selves, and our being born into love and peace and wholeness and potency, arises out of my experiences with physical substance

7

in the transformations of clay, out of my experiences of language, out of my dreams and my deeds, out of my sense of touch and my experience of death. Mystery sucks at our breath like a wind tunnel. Invites us into it. Let us pray, and enter.

Let no one think that the birth of man is to be felt without terror. The transformations that await us cost everything in the way of courage and sacrifice. Let no one be deluded that a knowledge of the path can substitute for putting one foot in front of the other. CENTERING, which I discuss in this book, is a severe and thrilling discipline, often acutely unpleasant. In my own efforts, I become weak, discouraged, exhausted, angry, frustrated, unhappy, and confused. But someone within me is resolute, and I try again. Within us lives a merciful being who helps us to our feet however many times we fall.

CHAPTER I

Centering as Dialogue

Centering: that act which precedes all others on the potter's wheel. The bringing of the clay into a spinning, unwobbling pivot, which will then be free to take innumerable shapes as potter and clay press against each other. The firm, tender, sensitive pressure which yields as much as it asserts. It is like a handclasp between two living hands, receiving the greeting at the very moment that they give it. It is this speech between the hand and the clay that makes me think of dialogue. And it is a language far more interesting than the spoken vocabulary which tries to describe it, for it is spoken not by the tongue and lips but by the whole body, by the whole person, speaking and listening. And with listening too, it seems to me, it is not the ear that hears, it is not the physical organ that performs that act of inner receptivity. It is the total person who hears. Sometimes the skin seems to be the best listener, as it prickles and thrills, say to a sound or a silence; or the fantasy, the imagination: how it bursts into inner pictures as it listens and then responds by pressing its language, its forms, into the listening clay. To be open to what we hear, to be open in what we say . . .

There is a joke that always amuses me whenever I think of it. You may know it too. A man and woman have stayed happily married for years. Nobody can understand how they do it. Everybody else is getting divorced or separated — suffering the agonies of marital estrangement. A friend asks the husband of the lucky pair how they have been able to make a go of it. What's the secret of their success? "Oh," answers the husband, "it's very simple. We simply divide up the household problems. My wife makes all the minor decisions and I make all the major decisions. No friction!" "I see," says the friend, "and what are the minor decisions your wife makes, for example; and the major decisions, which are they?" "Well," answers the husband, "my wife makes all the little decisions like where shall we send our son to college, shall we sell the house, should we renew our medical insurance, and, uh ... and then I take the big ones: like Should Red China Join the United Nations, Should the United States Disarm Unilaterally, Is Peace Possible ... ?"

I think this is a good joke because it takes a warm and humorous view of what is exactly the task of a marriage: a marriage of one person with another, or a marriage within one person of what seem to be separate concerns, and yet unless both are managed well, one's life or one's marriage tends to be wobbly indeed. Craftsmen live with a special immediacy in the double realms of these concerns: the questions of technique and the questions of meaning. Where shall I attach the handle to this pitcher? Shall I decorate this surface or let the clay stand clean? How thin? How thick? as well as What is a potter? What is the relation of pottery to poetry? What is the meaning of impermanence? When is a pot not a pot? What is freedom? What is originality? Are there rules?

I will now act as husband and wife to these dilemmas. I will answer these questions:

Where should I attach the handle to this pitcher? The question here lies in the "should." What does it mean, "should"? What kind of handle do I *want*? I don't know, I don't know. What does it mean, "I don't know"? It means that there are many different kinds of considerations, and I don't know how to satisfy them all. I want the handle to be strong enough to support the weight of the pitcher when it is filled. I want to be able to get my hand through it. I want it to be placed so that it does not weaken the wall and crack the pot, and so that the balance of the pitcher is good in pouring. I want it to make a beautiful total shape. I want it to be *my* handle at the same time that I want to please my customer, my friends, my critics, whomever. And in another impulse I don't care about any of these things: I want it to be a complete surprise. Poetry often enters through the window of irrelevance. So if the handle does not satisfy any of the above requirements, the pot may have a certain marvelous charm, an original image: a cracked pitcher that carries in it the magic of the self-forgetful impulse which in a rage of joy and irreverence stuck the handle on in something of the spirit in which we pin the tail on the donkey blindfolded. A glee, an energy, that escapes from all those questions-and-answers, thumbs its nose, stands on the ridgepole, and crows like a cock for its own dawning.

What is it all about? These different moods sweep through us. How much authority should we give them? To be solemn to be merry to be chaste to be voluptuous to be reserved to be prodigal to be elegant to be vulgar to be tasteful to be tasteless to be useful to be useless to be something to be nothing to be alive is to live in this weather.

A pot should this, and a pot should that — I have little patience with these prescriptions. I cannot escape paradox when I look deep into things, in the crafts as well as in poetry in metaphysics or in physics. In physics, matter is immaterial. The physical world, it turns out, is invisible, inaudible, immeasurable; supersensible and unpredictable. Law exists; and yet freedom is possible. In metaphysics, life and death in the commonplace sense collaborate in rhythms which sustain life. The birth of the new entails the death of the old, change; and yet the old does not literally die, it lives on, transformed. In ancient mystery religions, initiation for life required a ritual death. In poetry, in metaphor which is its instrument, the opposites also fuse: for example, I once wrote a very short poem, in the style of the Japanese haiku. It was entitled "Snow." And it went like this:

> White moths in crazy mobs
> hunt everywhere
> the flame of the winter sun.

Why do I write about moths and call the poem "Snow"? Snow is crystalline, mineral, inert. Moths are alive, fluttering, impelled. The snow melts in the sun, dies. Turns to water, symbol of life. In the swirling snow I see the realm of life, not with my senses but with what you might call my supersenses: supersensible life. Life seeking life, the sun. Seeking light. The cold seeking the warm. The instinct seeking its transformation. Physical weather as the image of the dance of life; the quest, even in the heart of winter; the glorious sun making us ecstatic to burn ourselves alive in its energy, to worship at the center.

At the center. Pottery as metaphysics. Centering. How all these thoughts and experiences create a sense of an enormous cosmic unity, a sense of a quiet inner unity, a unity within me, child of that vast single god-sea, that unity, wherein we swim. In pottery, as my first teacher Robert Turner said, the toughest thing to learn comes at the very beginning, if you are learning to throw on the potter's wheel. The centering of the clay. It took me seven years before I could, with certainty, center any given piece of clay. Another person might center the clay the first time he sat down to it. His task then might be to allow the centered clay to live into a form which it would itself declare. My task was to learn how to bring in the flying images, how to keep from falling in love with a mistake, how to bring the images in, down, up, smoothly, centered, and then to allow them the kind of breath they cannot have if all they know how to be is passionate or repressed.

But of course we have to be passionate. That is to say, when we are, we must be able to be. We must be able to let the intensity — the Dionysian rapture and disorder and the celebration of chaos, of potentiality, the experience of surrender — we must be able to let it live in our bodies, in our hands, through our hands into the materials we work with. I sense this: that we must be steady enough in ourselves, to be open and to let the winds of life blow through us, to be our breath, our inspiration; to breathe with them, mobile and soft in the limberness of our bodies, in our agility, our ability, as it were, to dance, and yet to stand upright, to be intact, to be persons. We come to know ourselves, and others, through the images we create in such moods. These images are disclosures of ourselves to ourselves. They are life-revelations. If we can stay "on center" and look with clear-seeing eyes and compassionate hearts at what we have done, we may advance in self-knowledge and in knowledge of our materials and of the world in its larger concerns.

The creative spirit creates with whatever materials are present. With food, with children, with building blocks, with speech, with thoughts, with pigment, with an umbrella, or a wineglass, or a torch. We are not craftsmen only during studio hours. Any more than a man is wise only in his library. Or devout only in church. The material is not the sign of the creative feeling for life: of the warmth and sympathy and reverence which foster being; techniques are not the sign; "art" is not the sign. The sign is the light that dwells within the act, whatever its nature or its medium.

Craft, as you may know, comes from the German word *Kraft*, meaning *power* or *strength*. As Emerson said, the law is: "Do the thing, and you shall have the power. But they who do not the thing, have not the powers." We can't fake craft. It lies in the act. The strains we have put in the clay break open in the fire. We do not have the craft, or craftsmanship, if we do not speak to the light that lives within the earthly materials; this means ALL earthly materials, including men themselves.

There is a wonderful legend in Jewish Hasidism that in the beginning when God poured out his grace, man was not able to stand firm before the fullness and the vessels

I 2

broke and sparks fell out of them into all things. And shells formed around them. By our hallowing, we may help to free these sparks. They lie everywhere, in our tools, in our food, in our clothes . . . A kind of radiance, an emanation, a freedom, something that fills our hearts with joy and gratitude no matter how it may strike our judgment! There is something within man that seeks this joy. That knows this joy. Joy is different from happiness. I am not talking about happiness. I am talking about joy. How, when the mind stops its circling, we say YES, YES to what we behold.

Another picture from which I draw inspiration: Robert Turner, sitting at the potter's wheel in our shop at Black Mountain College, giving a demonstration. He was centering the clay, and then he was opening it and pulling up the walls of the cylinder. He was not looking at the clay. He had his ear to it. He was listening. "It is breathing," he said; and then he filled it with air.

There are many marvelous stories of potters in ancient China. In one of them a noble is riding through a town and he passes a potter at work. He admires the pots the man is making: their grace and a kind of rude strength in them. He dismounts from his horse and speaks with the potter. "How are you able to form these vessels so that they possess such convincing beauty?" "Oh," answers the potter, "you are looking at the mere outward shape. What I am forming lies within. I am interested only in what remains after the pot has been broken."

It is not the pots we are forming, but ourselves. That is the husband's concern. The wife's: Will it hold water? Can I cook in it?

In a book entitled *Zen Flesh Zen Bones,* there is a section called "Centering." The editor, Paul Reps, tells us it is a transcription of ancient Sanskrit manuscripts. It presents teaching, still alive in Kashmir and parts of India after more than four thousand years, that may well be the roots of Zen Buddhism. The editor, plainly reserving for himself the major questions, ends his introduction with these words: "The problem of our mind, relating conscious to preconscious awareness, takes us deep into everyday living. Dare we open our doors to the source of our being? What are flesh and bones for?"

I am a question-asker and a truth-seeker. I do not have much in the way of status in my life, nor security. I have been on quest, as it were, from the beginning. For a long time I thought there was something wrong with me: no ambition, no interest in tenure, always on the march, changing every seven years, from landscape to landscape. Certain elements were constant: the poetry, the desire for relationship, the sense of voyage. But lately I have developed also a sense of destination, or destiny. And a sense that if I am to be on quest, I must expect to live like a pilgrim; I must keep to the inner path. I must be able to be whoever I am.

For example, it seemed strange to me, as to others, that, having taken my Ph.D. in English, I should then in the middle of my life, instead of taking up a college professorship, turn to the art of pottery. During one period, when people asked me what I did, I was uncertain what to answer; I guessed I could say I taught English, wrote poetry, and made pottery. What was my occupation? I finally gave up and said "Person."

Having been imbued with the ordinary superstitions of American higher education, among which is the belief that something known as the life of the mind is more apt to take you where you want to go than any other kind of life, I busied myself with learning to practice logic, grammar, analysis, summary, generalization; I learned to make distinctions, to speculate, to purvey information. I was educated to be an intellectual of the verbal type. I might have been a philosophy major, a literature major, a language major. I was always a kind of oddball even in undergraduate circles, as I played kick-goal on the Reed College campus with President Dexter Keezer. And in graduate school, even more so. Examinations tended to make me merry, often seeming to me to be some kind of private game, some secret ritual compulsively played by the professors and the institution. I invariably became facetious in all the critical hours. All that solemnity for a few facts! I couldn't believe they were serious. But they were. I never quite understood it. But I loved the dream and the reality that lay behind those texts and in the souls of my teachers. I often felt like a kind of fraud, because I suspected that the knowledge I was acquiring and being rewarded for by academic diploma was wide wide of the truth I sensed to live somewhere, somewhere. I felt that I knew little of real importance; and when would the day come that others would realize it too, and I would be exposed? I have had dream after dream in which it turns out that I have not really completed my examinations for the doctorate and have them still to pass. And I sweat with anxiety. A sense of occupying a certain position without possessing the real thing: the deeper qualifications of wisdom and prophecy. But of course it was not the world who exposed me, it was my dreams. I do not know if I am a philosopher, but if philosophy is the love of wisdom, then I am a philosopher, because I love wisdom and that is why I love the crafts, because they are wise.

I became a teacher quite by chance. Liked it, found in education an image through which I could examine the possibilities of growth, of nourishment, of the experiences that lead to knowledge of nature and of self. It was a good trade to be in if you were a question-asker.

But the trouble was that though the work absorbed my mind, it used very little else. And I am by now convinced that wisdom is not the product of mental effort. Wisdom is a state of the total being, in which capacities for knowledge and for love, for survival and for death, for imagination, inspiration, intuition, for all the fabulous functioning of this human being who we are, come into a center with their forces, come into an experience of meaning that can voice itself as wise action. It is not enough to belong to a Society of Friends who believe in non-violence if, when frustrated, your body spontaneously contracts and shoots out its fist to knock another man down. It is in our bodies that redemption takes place. It is the physicality of the crafts that pleases me: I learn through my hands and my eyes and my skin what I could never learn through my brain. I develop a sense of life, of the world of earth, air, fire, and water — and wood, to add the fifth element according to Oriental alchemy — which could be developed in no other way. And if it is life I am fostering, I must maintain a kind of dialogue with the clay, listening, serving, interpreting as well as mastering. The union of our wills, like a marriage, it is a beautiful act, the act of centering and turning a pot on the potter's wheel; and the sexual images implicit in the forming of the cone and opening of the vessel are archetypal; likewise the give-and-take in the forming of a pot out of slabs, out of raw shards, out of coils; the union of natural intelligences: the intelligence of the clay, my intelligence, the intelligence of the tools, the intelligence of the fire.

You don't need me to tell you what education is. Everybody really knows that education goes on all the time everywhere all through our lives, and that it is the process of waking up to life. Jean Henri Fabre said something just about like that, I think. He said that to be educated was not to be taught but to wake up. It takes a heap of resolve to keep from going to sleep in the middle of the show. It's not that we want to sleep our lives away. It's that it requires certain kinds of energy, certain capacities for taking the world into our consciousness, certain real powers of body and soul to be a match for reality. That's why knowledge and consciousness are two quite different things. Knowledge is like a product we consume and store. All we need are good closets. By consciousness I mean a state of being "awake" to the world throughout our organism. This kind of consciousness requires not closets but an organism attuned to the finest perceptions and responses. It allows experience to breathe through it as light enters and changes a room. When knowledge is transformed into consciousness and into will, ah then we are on the high road indeed . . .

That which we consume, with a certain passivity, accepting it for the most part from our teachers, who in turn have accepted it from theirs, is like the food we eat. And food, in order to become energy, or will, is transformed entirely by the processes of metabolism. We do not become the food we eat. Rather the food turns into us. Similarly with knowledge, at best. Hopefully, we do not turn into encyclopedias or propaganda machines or electric brains. Our knowledge, if we allow it to be transformed within us, turns into capacity for life-serving human deeds. If knowledge does not turn into life, it makes cripples and madmen and dunces. It poisons just as food would if it stayed in the stomach and was never digested, and the waste products never thrown off.

It is dangerous to seek to possess knowledge, as if it could be stored. For one thing, it tends to make one impatient with ignorance, as people busy with money-seeking tend to be impatient with idlers. Though ignorance is the prime prerequisite for education, many teachers appear offended by it — or worse, contemptuous. Perhaps it is partly for this reason that many prefer to give advanced courses to select or "gifted" groups.

The possession of knowledge may create a materialism of its own. Knowledge becomes property. Teachers compete with each other for status, wealth, influence. A professor of education was speaking to friends of education in the county where I live, and she was urging pay raises as bait for hiring good teachers, "for after all, the standard of success is the salary check." Naturally in this climate professional educators are apt to quarrel over tactics and to engage in pressure politics, motivated by a desire to protect their security and to establish their views as ruling policy. In other words, education may be sacrificed to knowledge-as-commodity. Just as life is sometimes sacrificed to art-as-arrangement. The quest is abandoned. Instead, property is bought at the site of the last dragon killed, and a ruling class is formed out of the heroes. The knights grow fat and lazy and conceited and petulant. They parade in their armor on special occasions to bedazzle the populace. But in their hearts are terror and duplicity. And when difficult times come, they fall upon each other with their rusty axes and try to divide the world into those who know and those who don't. There is nothing to equal in bitterness and gall, childish-

16

ness and spite, the intramural warfare of the academic community. Where is honor? Where is devotion? Where is responsibility of soul?

Such an atmosphere brought me gradually to imagine possible shortcomings in the educational system I had docilely trusted. Initiative and imagination seemed sorely lacking. Teachers seemed to apply to their students the same pressures that had crippled them. Most of us have been brain-washed to think that knowledge and security make the world go round. And if the world seems to be going round very poorly, we do not think of questioning deeply its education. The need for creative imagination in the intellectually trained person is drastic. Also the need for spontaneous human feeling.

Fashionable thinking may dominate the scientist and artist and scholar alike. For them, knowledge is the body of facts currently in fashion. Art is the image and compositional practice now in fashion. Since it is difficult to test the truth of most facts, faculty and students alike settle for "interesting," "original," and "self-consistent" theories. An ability to marshal and interpret "evidence" is highly esteemed, though evidence is often no more than opinions strongly held or secondary research. Very little stress is placed on developing powers of observation or on intuition. Thus, with primary experience held so at a distance, sensory life in particular, I find that my principal task in teaching adults is to win their trust. They tend to be overwhelmingly oriented to manipulation and to effect. It rarely occurs to them to work in a direct way with what they know and are. Their primary motivations are to please, to make a strong impression, to do either what is expected (if they are docile) or what is unexpected (if they are hostile). They assume that pretense and falsity are virtues. The whole thing sometimes seems like a massive confidence game.

Like other men, teachers tend to withhold themselves from naked personal contact. They tend to pin their hopes on jargon and style. And this, I have observed, is what many students learn from them: afraid to reveal themselves, burdened with shame and dismay and hopelessness, or expertise and cunning.

A theory much in vogue is that Western man is sick with sexual repression and pleasure anxiety. I believe that the squelching of the "person" and his spontaneous intuitive response to experience is as much at the root of our timidity, our falseness. Teachers and students who in the great school markets barter their learning for salaries and grades are hungry for respect, for personal relationship, for warmth. Unfortunately,

17

they have the impression that these are extracurricular (like Newton's secondary qualities of color and so on) — and their capacity for balance between the life within and the world without shrinks or falters, or their desperation turns rank.

It is a sensitive matter, of course. I am not going to all these words merely to insult the spirit of true research. But my life as a teacher and as a member of the human community advises me that education may estrange us from life-commitment as well as bind us firmly within it. There are all kinds of things to learn, and we had best learn them all. One of the reasons formal education is in danger today is that a sense of work is split off from human earnestness. How may this split be healed? Working with our materials as artist-craftsmen may help to engender a new health here.

An act of the self, that's what one must make. An act of the self, from me to you. From center to center. We must mean what we say, from our innermost heart to the outermost galaxy. Otherwise we are lost and dizzy in a maze of reflections. We carry light within us. There is no need merely to reflect. Others carry light within them. These lights must wake to each other. My face is real. Yours is. Let us find our way to our initiative.

For must we not show ourselves to each other, and will we not know then who are the teachers and who are the students? Do we not all learn from one another? My students at City College are worldly-wise and naïve as lambs. I am sophisticated and uninformed. We make a good combination. They have never heard of e. e. cummings, who lived in their city, nor of the New York painters. They do not know that there are free art galleries where they may see the latest works of modern artists. They do not know very much about contemporary "culture." But they know well the life of the subway, the office, the factory, the union hall, the hassle for employment; they know what they did in the war or in their escape from Hungary or Germany, or in occupied France, or Israel. They know what it is like to be black in America. They are patient with my obtuseness, they check my too quick judgments, my sarcasm which is unperceptive. I help them to unmask, to be openly as tender and hopeful and generous as they inwardly are. I help them to open themselves to knowledge. They help me to open myself to life. We are equal in courage.

Must weakness be concealed in order that respect be won? Must love and fervor be concealed? Must we pretend to fearlessness? and certainty? Surely education should equip us to know what to fear and what to be uncertain of. Surely it should equip us in personal honor.

18

Must. Should. Convenient words! Exhortations meant to loosen the grip of congealed behavior . . . Perhaps these perceptions are not the proper work of intellect, but of some other faculty deeply neglected in our education. In any case, at a critical moment in life my hunger for nakedness and realism and nobility turned to the clay of earth itself, and to water and fire.

I took up pottery also, in a sense, by chance. Unforeseen opportunity joined with interest and readiness. Like teaching, not a consciously sought but surely a destined union. For the materials and processes of pottery spoke to me of cosmic presences and transformations quite as surely as the pots themselves enchanted me. Experiences of the plastic clay and the firing of the ware carried more than commonplace values. Joy resonated deep within me, and it has stirred these thoughts only slowly to the surface. I have come to feel that we live in a universe of spirit, which materializes and de-materializes grandly; all things seem to me to live, and all acts to contain meaning deeper than matter-of-fact; and the things we do with deepest love and interest compel us by the spiritual forces which dwell in them. This seems to me to be a dialogue of the visible and the invisible to which our ears are attuned.

There was, first of all, something in the nature of the clay itself. You can do very many things with it, push this way and pull that, squeeze and roll and attach and pinch and hollow and pile. But you can't do everything with it. You can go only so far, and then the clay resists. To know ourselves by our resistances — this is a thought first expressed to me by the poet Charles Olson.

And so it is with persons. You can do very many things with us: push us together and pull us apart and squeeze us and roll us flat, empty us out and fill us up. You can surround us with influences, but there comes a point when you can do no more. The person resists, in one way or another (if it is only by collapsing, like the clay). His own will becomes active.

This is a wonderful moment, when one feels his will become active, come as a force into the total assemblage and dynamic intercourse and interpenetration of will impulses. When one stands like a natural substance, plastic but with one's own character written into the formula, ah then one feels oneself part of the world, taking one's shape with its help — but a shape only one's own freedom can create.

And the centering of the clay, of which I have spoken. The opening of the form. And the firing of the pot. This experience has deep psychic reverberations: how the pot, which was originally plastic, sets into dry clay, brittle and fragile, and then by being heated to a certain temperature hardens into stone. By natural law as it were, it takes its final form. Ordeal by fire. Then, the form once taken, the pot may not last, the body may perish; but the inner form has been taken, and it cannot break in the same sense.

I, like everyone I know, am instinctively motivated toward symbols of wholeness. What is a simpler, more natural one than the pot fired? Wholeness may be thought of as a kind of inner equilibrium, in which all our capacities have been brought into functioning as an organism. The potencies of the whole organism flow into the gestures of any part. And the sensation in any part reverberates throughout the soul. The unconscious and conscious levels of being can work together at the tasks of life, conveying messages to each other, assimilating one another. In wholeness I sense an integration of those characteristics which are uniquely ME and those interests which I share with the rest of mankind. As for example any bowl is symbolic of an archetypal circular form, which I share with all, but which I make and which therefore contains those very qualities of myself which are active in the making. I believe that pots have the smell of the person who makes them: a smell of tenderness, of vanity or ambition, of ease and naturalness, of petulance, uncertainty, callousness, fussiness, playfulness, solemnity, exuberance, absent-mindedness. The pot gives off something. It gives off its innerness, that which it holds but which cannot be seen.

In pottery, by developing sensitivity in manipulating natural materials by hand, I found a wisdom which had died out of the concepts I learned in the university: abstractions, mineralized and dead; while the minerals themselves were alive with energy and meaning. The life I found in the craft helped to bring to a new birth my ideals in education. Some secret center became vitalized in those hours of silent practice in the arts of transformation.

The experience of centering was one I particularly sought because I thought of myself as dispersed, interested in too many things. I envied people who were "single-minded," who had one powerful talent and who knew when they got up in the morning what it was they had to do. Whereas I, wherever I turned, felt the enchantment: to the window for the sweetness of the air; to the door for the passing figures; to the teapot, the typewriter, the knitting needles, the pets, the pottery, the newspaper, the telephone. Wherever I looked, I could have lived.

It took me half my life to come to believe I was OK even if I did love experience in a loose and undiscriminating way and did not know for sure the difference between good and bad. My struggles to accept my nature were the struggles of centering. I found myself at odds with the propaganda of our times. One is supposed to be either an artist or a homemaker, by one popular superstition. Either a teacher or a poet, by a theory which says that poetry must not sermonize. Either a craftsman or an intellectual, by a snobbism which claims either hand or head as the seat of true power. One is supposed to concentrate and not to spread oneself thin, as the jargon goes. And this is a jargon spoken by a cultural leadership from which it takes time to win one's freedom, if one is not lucky enough to have been born free. Finally, I hit upon an image: a seed-sower. Not to worry about which seeds sprout. But to give them as my gift in good faith.

But in spite of my self-acceptance, I still clung to a concept of purity which was chaste and aloof from the fellowship of man, and had yet to center the image of a pure heart in whose bright warm streams the world is invited to bathe. A heart who can be touched and who stirs in response, bringing the whole body into an act of greeting.

Well then, I became a potter.

And I found that the mute arts of the craftsman's world combine fruitfully with the verbal arts of the teacher or poet. For what is poetry anyway, and teaching? In order to teach, you must be able to listen. You must be able to hear what the person before you means. You cannot assume the meanings and be a teacher; you must enter again into a dialogue — with all senses alert to the human meanings expressed, however implicitly. The experience of the potter listening to his clay strengthens this capacity. One must be able to hear the inner questions, the unspoken ones; the inner hopes and misgivings and dreams and timidities and potentialities and stupidities. One must listen carefully in order to serve as a proper midwife to the birth of consciousness in the student. The world is always bigger than one's own focus. And as we bring ourselves into center wherever we are, the more of that world we can bring into service, the larger will be the capacity of our action and our understanding. The more sensitivity and courage I develop working with clay and water and mineral pigments and fire, the more helpful I can be to my Negro

21

student from Panama who is taking freshman composition. All teachers should, as part of their class preparation, practice an art.

And the poetry. What is poetry: poetry is truth; and what is truth: truth is reality; and what is reality: reality is nature; and what is nature (you see what a good husband I am, asking all these Important Questions and answering them!): nature is life; and what is life: life is a death-dance; and what is a death-dance: a death-dance is the casting off of the corpse and the eating of the flame: the flame enters the womb, the green flame flickers in the seed, the new being is born, the next moment, the unfolding mystery. All the forces of the mineral world, in our skeleton as it were, all that salt and calcium and whatever it all is, want to grow rigid, want to congeal; all our habits and learned ignorance weigh us down; the death-dance burns away the bone, burns away, and lets the living impulses rise, the vision rise. Poetry tells the truth. But it doesn't invent the truth. It too must listen, to the poetry that flows inaudibly beneath all speech. So it is difficult to use words and yet to invoke the sense of life which is unspoken, unspeakable, what is left after the books are all decayed, lost, burned, forgotten. What remains after the pot has disappeared.

Pottery has helped my poetry because I was less instructed in the handcraft and therefore less inhibited. I permitted myself a kind of freedom in the use of clay which I would not have known how to find in the verbal world. The freedom I experienced in my studio began to drift into my study.

Well, and what is freedom? First of all, freedom seems to mean the absence of external restraint, the freedom to play. When we are free from external tyrannies, we seek freedom from our inner limitations. We find that in order to play we must be nimble and flexible and imaginative, we must be able to have fun, we must *feel* enjoyment, and sometimes long imprisonment has made us numb and sluggish. And then we find out that there are, paradoxically, disciplines which create in us capacities which allow us to seek our freedom. We learn how to rid ourselves of our boredom, our stiffness, our repressed anger, our anxiety. We become brighter, more energy flows through us, our limbs rise, our spirit comes alive in our tissues. And our gratitude is immeasurable for all the hours of labor that carry us forward.

As I grow quiet, the clay centers. For example, I used to grieve because I could not make reliably a close-fitting lid for a canister, a teapot, a casserole. Sometimes the lid fitted, sometimes it didn't. But I wanted it to fit. And I was full of aggravation. Then a GI friend of mine who was stationed in Korea sent me an ancient Korean pot, about a thousand years old. I loved it at once, and then he wrote that he thought I might like it because it looked like something I might have made. Its lid didn't fit at all! Yet it was a museum piece, so to speak. Why, I mused, do I require of myself what I do not require of this pot? Its lid does not fit, but it inspires my spirit when I look at it and handle it. So I stopped worrying. Now I have very little trouble making lids that fit.

What I want to say is that as our personal universes expand, if we keep drawing ourselves into center again and again, everything seems to enhance everything else. It becomes unnecessary to choose which person to be as we open and close the same ball of clay. We will make pots for our English classes. Read poems to our pottery classes. Write on the clay, print from the clay. The activity seems to spring out of the same source: poem or pot, loaf of bread, letter to a friend, a morning's meditation, a walk in the woods, turning the compost pile, knitting a pair of shoes, weeping with pain, fainting with discouragement, burning with shame, trembling with indecision: what's the difference. I like especially two famous Zen stories: the one about the great Japanese master of the art of archery who had never in his life hit the bull's eye. And the other about the monk who said, "Now that I'm enlightened, I'm just as miserable as ever."

What I mean here is that in poetry, in pottery, in the life of the mind, it seems to me that one must be able to picture before oneself the opposite of what one has just declared in order to keep alive the possibility of freedom, of mobility, of growth. As soon as we find ourselves spellbound by order and our ability to control our medium and our tools, to do exactly what we want, we must do the opposite as well. As soon as we feel drunk with the sport of building and destroying, of forming in order to deform, of working unconsciously, with risk (with poetry, if poetry is saying hello to whoever-whatever is there): with danger, and disrespect for the canons of taste, do the opposite. One does not decide between craft and art, pottery and sculpture, tradition and the individual talent. One is in a perpetual dialogue and performs the act one performs.

Life leads us at a certain moment to step beyond the dualisms to which we have been educated: primitive and civilized, chaos and order, abnormal and normal, private and public, verbal and non-verbal, conventional and far-out, good and bad. To transform our tuitions, as Emerson called our learning, into the body of our intuitions so that we may use this body as in pottery we use our clay. By an act of centering we resolve the oppositions

23

in a single experience. The surrealists in France called it *le point suprème* and found it also at the center: *le foyer central*. When the sense of life in the individual is *in touch with* the life-power in the universe, is turning with it, he senses himself as potentially whole. And he senses all his struggles as efforts toward that wholeness. And he senses that wholeness as implicit in every part. When we are working on the potter's wheel, we are touching the clay at only one point; and yet as the pot turns through our fingers, the whole is being affected, and we have an experience of this wholeness. "The still point of the turning world."

Most of the separations we make need to be looked at very carefully: weakness and strength, sickness and health, not-knowing and knowing, play and seriousness. Human beings are an odd breed. We find it so difficult to give in to possibility — to envision what is not visible. For example, we tend to think that strength is all-important, and yet we have a very shallow notion of what strength consists of. For unless our weaknesses play into our strengths we are not as supple as we should be. And with our fixation upon health, we would do well to listen to the story that sickness is telling, as it brings its truth into our work. We must fill our devotion with the spirit of play, of celebration and holiday. Love-play. The rhythms of work seem to be the natural rhythms of life: they seem to go by polarities which swing around that unmoving center: the very rhythms of our breathing are the dialogue of inner and outer. The single craftsman finding his own way, and the same craftsman seeking fellowship with others. Working by preliminary design is answered by a desire to improvise. The joy of producing a well-made pot, beautiful in its physical balance and grace and accurate in its usefulness, is answered by a kinship with the ambiguous: some image which fills us with wonder or mirth or which leads us into continuous exercise of our faculties in an effort to fathom it, to grasp it, to embrace it. For we must surely embrace our world. Unless our ideals of peace and of love are so much cant, we must surely embrace our world in all its daily happenings and details.

What is the purpose of thinking about it in this way? Well, lots of folks worry about what things are called. Is it craft? is it art? is it sculpture? is it dada? is it music? is it noise? is it poetry? *what is it*? The words people use won't change anything (I'm not absolutely sure of this). Certainly these words of mine won't change anything. And the worrying has its own function to perform. Life changes things. If there are life and truth in anybody's words, OK. Then they will correspond with nature. And if we are going along with nature, we will not need to be *told* anything. The Buddha, you may recall, came to speak to a gathering, and he used no words. He held a flower up before the people.

"Poetry," said Wallace Stevens, "is a process of the personality of the poet." Creative work is a training of each individual's perception according to the level on which he is alive and awake; that is why it is so difficult to evaluate. And it should be difficult. In art, perception is embodied: in dust, in pigment, in sounds, in movements of the body, in metals and stone, in threads and stuffs. Each product, each goal, is an intermediate moment in a much longer journey of the person. Once when I was asked to write something about art, I wrote: "Art is an intuitive act of the spirit in its evolution toward divine nature." Because it is an act of self-education in this sense, it cannot be evaluated apart from its maker, the one whose vision it represents. That is why judging is such a ticklish business. To judge prematurely is often to cripple. To refrain from judging is sometimes to impoverish. One must, again, listen with one's total faculties before one speaks. For answers to questions of technique are, at another level, answers to questions of personal growth. The "minor" questions: How shall I make this lid, what kind of a handle shall I pull, how high a foot shall I throw on this pot, how small an opening should this bottle have, how much iron oxide shall I apply to this surface? — all these minor questions are the echoes and small ripples from the deeper questions: What am I doing? what do I know? what do I want to learn? how shall I bring myself into ripeness? Teachers of ourselves, we over and over again ask, "How do I want this to look?" And what we mean is, "What do I want to bring to birth in the world? In myself?" Our pots do bear our spirits into the world. We may then, it seems to me, let them grow like wild flowers, in all their varieties. But in our own gardens we may foster those which bring into our lives the influences we long for. We may also judge according to standards derived from the highest development we have observed.

My answer to the question, What shall I do about this handle or this lid? is — and I quote from that ancient text on "Centering" — "Wherever your attention alights, at this very point, *experience*." Make dozens, now this way, now that; putting them now here, now there. The *should* enters only when the goal is fixed, the standards formulated, and the techniques refined. Few of our moments have this character.

In teaching pottery, I am continually aware of how the learning of a handcraft reverberates throughout the spiritual organism, and it is this sense of personal destiny at

2 5

stake which makes teaching such a serious and stimulating endeavor. I wish now to speak of two friends whom I taught only briefly but whose experiences were especially meaningful to me in the terms I have been using here: two people in whose personal transformation craft played its part. One, an English teacher who had never before in her life touched a piece of raw clay with any hope of forming it, was imprisoned by fear and striving. The other, a college art teacher, more skillful than I on the potter's wheel, was impotent with ambition and conceit.

The beginner, a person of deep culture and intuition, did indeed listen, but with such tension that she could hardly hear; and she was tongue-tied in her own behalf. "Is that all right?" she would ask quaveringly. She touched each hunk of clay as if at any moment she might plunge through the bottom into the abyss. Everything seemed alarming, and delicious. Her body sought the contact, but her taste reproved the appearance. Finally I asked her to work with her eyes closed so that her hands could be liberated from the censure of her critically trained eyes. To let the pleasure and search and sinew for making grow a little bit before chastizing their immaturity. To do all the things that hands can do: tear and swat and push and pinch and squeeze and caress and scratch and model and beat. She sat like a blind woman with her clay, and she made a bowl this way, and when she opened her eyes, delight preceded doubt, and she was that much stronger in herself to do it again. She began to understand how it was for *her* to say if it was all right, not for me. I encouraged her to buy a can of workable clay and take it to her apartment. Her eyes are tired from reading. Let the hands carry forward the education.

Now the other potter had the opposite agony. He worked well, and produced in the beginning a regular storm of pots. But the more he did, the more he drooped. I heard he was going to drop pottery and take up weaving. One night I stood beside him at the wedging board while he morosely kneaded and slapped his clay. Suddenly he spoke. "What is a potter?" His accomplishment meant nothing to him. He did not LIKE his pots. They bore no individual stamp, he said. They did not speak to him. (Perhaps he had not spoken to them?) "What should a potter do?" he asked me. What should he make? Who should a potter be? (You see these are real questions that men do ask!) Well, I don't remember what I said, probably something about how a potter is a person; what should a person do? who should a person be? I suggested that he take a vacation from these thoughts of "should" — make some clay balloons and take them down to the granite sea shore and roll them on the lichen-textured boulders, and have some fun. He did that, and made a charming little stoneware garden. Although he didn't know exactly what to think about it, he liked it. But his troubles were by no means over. He did for awhile give up pottery and take up weaving. I heard later that during the rest of the summer he gradually came back to center and worked with the clay in a way that brought more and more of himself into it, so that he felt good.

We have to trust these feelings. We have to trust the invisible gauges we carry within us. We have to realize that a creative being lives within ourselves, whether we like it or not, and that we must get out of its way, for it will give us no peace until we do. Certain kinds of egotism and ambition as well as certain kinds of ignorance and timidity have to be overcome or they will stand in the way of that creator. And though we are well thought of by others, we will feel cross and frustrated and envious and petulant, as if we had been cheated, somehow, by life.

I cannot talk about the crafts without appealing to the evolving spirit of man. We grow and change and develop capacities for centering and for dialogue throughout our lives.

Part of the training we enjoy as craftsmen is to bring into our bodies the imagination and the will. We enact. The handcrafts stand to perpetuate the living experience of contact with natural elements — something primal, immediate, personal, material, a dialogue between our dreams and the forces of nature.

In pottery it is perhaps because of the fire that the sense of collaboration is so strong. The potter does everything he can do. But he cannot burst into flame and reach a temperature of 2300 degrees Fahrenheit for a period varying from eight hours to a week and harden plastic clay into rigid stone, and transform particles of silica and spar into flowing glaze. He cannot transmute the dull red powder that lies upon the biscuited ware into a light-responsive celadon. He can only surrender his ware to the fire, listen to it, talk to it, so that he and the fire respond to each other's power, and the fired pot is the child.

Some craftsmen seem to be troubled by the question of originality and imitation. My only standard here is that a person be led into a deeper experience of himself and his craft. Human beings learn by imitation; certainly, in the years of childhood, almost exclusively by imitation. One is inspired by someone else's example. One seeks to do likewise. Sometimes the effort to do likewise gradually creates capacities and perceptions that one did not feel before. These periods of imitation are usually temporary. They too may be aspects of the long journey each one of us is on to get where we are bound for, consciously or unconsciously. I have found imitation useful both as a discipline and as a momentary indulgence. People bring each other into activity. If, however, the phase of imitation congeals and one sticks in it out of inertia, then of course the works will begin to look tired too. Ideas do not belong to people. Ideas live in the world as we do. We discover certain ideas at certain times. Someone enjoys a certain revelation and passes it around. A certain person's courage inspires a similar courage in others. People share their culture: there are enjoyable resemblances that make us feel like a community of fellow beings, fellow craftsmen — using a tradition and contributing our own impulses to it.

I have a finger exercise for originality which I sometimes use. Working with a piece of clay, hand-building, I destroy every pleasing result, seeking the unrecognizable. For if it is new, it will not look like something else: not like driftwood nor a Henry Moore perforated torso, not like a coral reef nor a Giacometti sculpture, not like a Haniwa horse nor a madonna nor a "free form," nor the new look in pottery in the 'sixties. It will look very odd indeed, if it is really new. Insecurity we need perhaps the most when we are inventing: it seems like our philosopher's stone, turning base materials into gold. The image we make in such an exercise will not be our goal, but in creating it we will have performed acts for the first time, and these will bring new structures and coordinations into our hands and into our visions.

In my own work I like to vary my rhythms: from one of a kind to many of a kind. Two sayings from that ancient tract on CENTERING make one passage of my dialogue: "Wherever satisfaction is found, in whatever act, *actualize this*"; and "Just as you have the impulse to do something, stop."

I admire very much the pottery of Karen Karnes, with whom I share a shop in Stony Point, New York. Her work is clean, expert, uncluttered, useful, beautiful, restrained but warm, full of a feeling of original plasticity as well as the advantages of stone. A plastic form with beautifully fitted rims. And the shiny glazes of high heat. Yet my temperament turns equally to ornament, to fooling around, to doing I know not what. And to letting the clay stand naked and untreated. Or any combination of these, at any moment of their intersection. I like a dry scabby surface through which color barely strains as well as depths soaked in lustre. Or just a simple semiglossy easily washable surface, no high jinks. The more a piece confounds me, the more it interests me. At the same time, one of the most thrilling experiences for me is to make table ware: twelve plates of the same size, twelve cups, twelve bowls. One after another. To make a lot of things alike is as exciting as to make one surprise after another. And of course the rewards of sustained working rhythms are marvelous. To throw forty tea bowls and to feel that certain ones have *it*. Have *mu*. Have *shibui*. Then you throw all the others away? No. For the quality of magic is not that clear: where you had been slowest to detect it, there it suddenly stands.

And yet the opposite is also true. There are moments when I could with ease clear all the shelves, clear the board, all the past, plough it under, make it new. Throw everything away. Is this a paradox? To be in love with the material world in all its stages of imperfection and yet to feel that love does not depend upon the permanence of its images? It is not the images per se that we adore but the being who lives within them and will live after the pot is broken. So goes the weather of this love of life and love of death, the feeling that the living and the dead are a permanent family fully alive in an awesome cosmic dialogue.

During the dozen years that I have been working with clay, certain influences from the potter's world have inspired me in special ways. The French potters in Vallauris. The folk potters in North Carolina, living by their craft, producing every day quantities of their unselfconscious simple useful appealing ware. Bernard Leach, as person, as potter, as author of *A Potter's Book, Potter's Portfolio, Potter in Japan*. Raku ware: the Japanese-derived ceremony of making a cup, firing it, and drinking tea out of it, all in a single rhythm: the living relation of the shaping and the drinking and the consecration. Bizen ware. Children who come into my studio to fool around with my clay. Three teachers: Warren McKenzie, fresh from a stint at St. Ives Pottery in England, where he had had to make five hundred mugs before the first one was accepted. Daniel Rhodes, his love for the craft in all the richness of its history and the combination in him of knowledge and feeling. Peter Voulkos, who told me to work with the clay till it collapses, that there's nothing to it, that if pots weren't breakable potters would be sunk, that there's lots more where these come from. Exhibitions of work in clay by sculptors Noguchi and Marisol and Nakian; exhibits at Asia House from Oriental antiquity and the present day; a visit to Mexico, all that carved stone and all that clay; a visit to Picasso's ceramics in Antibes; Henry Takemoto's coiled pots big enough to hide a thief; the paper-thin poetry of Lucy Rie's thrown porcelain.

But perhaps most vivid: a visit to this country by a Japanese potter, Rosanjin. He gave a speech at Greenwich House in New York City. In Japanese. He smiled throughout, and spoke with feeling. At the end, a young lady read an English translation. He began, she said, by saying how glad he was to be here, and how much he had enjoyed looking around the Greenwich House pottery at the potters' work, and how he couldn't help wondering why they all made such hideous things! A great evening . . . He spoke about educating one's feeling through a close relationship with nature and through drawing nature and studying the masterpieces of previous ages. Then he gave a demonstration. A potter's wheel was on stage. He did not throw the cylinder, he asked one of the visiting professors to do that. Rosanjin pinched its wall, turned to his translator, and said, "The clay is too wet, but I'll see what I can do with it." He then shaped a bowl. But because he opened it too wide for the wetness of the clay, it collapsed. Then he rolled fat coils between his hands and, lifting the rim of the fallen pot, propped it up. He pinched the rim into ripples and held this extraordinary flop before his horrified audience of American studio potters for admiration. Not only that, but he had it carried through the hall, up one row and down the next, to be examined and enjoyed. His smiling comment was, "It doesn't look like much now, but wait till the fire gets through with it, you never can tell!" I was transported with delight and mirth and admiration. American pieties were being offended right and left. The Orient was with us. Bringing its own joyful reverence, its own pieties to speak with ours.

David Tudor is not a potter but a pianist. He came to Black Mountain College one summer to give concerts. A half-dozen young student composers had arranged a short program of their works and, not being performers, asked him if he would play. I will never forget it. A grand piano. A college dining hall. All of us in blue jeans and tee shirts. The pianist in a sports jacket to lend a formal air. He entered from the "wings" with each small score, played the piece, whatever it was, with absolute sincerity and respect for the composer and the composed; bowed, exited, re-entered. A half-dozen compositions by beginners, handled without reservation nor irony nor sentiment nor anything except the capacity to let the moment *speak,* and us *listen.* Is this not the emptiness for which the sages pray: to be filled as a spring is?

I have been inspired as well by potters who undertake huge tasks and realize them faultlessly. I once saw Mary Scheier throw bowls. Huge beautiful curved thin instruments: like bells. All the clay used and the bowl soaring off the wheel like a bubble.

And Margaret Israel's exhibition of works in clay at the Egan Gallery in New York during the winter of 1961. No pots. All sculpture. Mythic, archetypal, musing, bemused images. Huge impossible forms, all hand built; huge sacks, like grain sacks, made of clay, standing empty in the corner. Caves with rose windows and congregations. A horse's muzzle and a woman's face, emerging out of a clay union, into physiognomy. A book with clay pages. A doorway, eight feet high. A boulder too big to fit in a kiln. A box, with an axis, with an altar, with gears. And I learned that the potter came every day to change something. To smudge a little soot on here and there, to alter the color of the body. To try a little blue paint. To remove a figure, to add a figure, to break something. To put something on a pedestal, to take something off. Chaos still bubbling and seething with possibilities. And the frenzied artist carbonated with creative impulses.

To tear this one down so that we can put this one up. But *we* don't have to do it. Life and time do it. And we discover that what is being created is a single being: its apparent lives and deaths only the appearances of its metamorphosis.

Life in both its outward crafts and inner forms offers us the experience of destruction and creation. We speak in a vocabulary that discriminates between meaningful form and lack of form, between pot and shard. At the same time we cultivate a love for each particular thing, each particular moment, no matter where it stands in the long rhythms of life and death: I have an ancient Egyptian potsherd mounted on my treasure shelf. We discover that now is always alive, and that the generative force within life continuously heals what appear to be separations, by making them fruitful. It is an important thing for us to cherish this living contact, finding through it our poetry, our pots, our love for each other and for life: the centering and the dialogue.

I tried once to put this impression into a poem:

Poem

Pots are for shards,
                    and
shards are
            for shepherds, to cry with.
SHAPES. taken, and taking
shape:
            avoid it if you can, you can't,
            shape's the void
            we're in; order is
            the chaos we befriend.
                              SAMSARA: one
thing and not another, one thing
and then another; samsara, is what
it's called, what we're at and what we're
in: forms, and naming. Names we bandy and
are scouted by, th'outs and innings, everyday a
requiem-birthday,
            spilling the shepherd's tears, spoiling the shep-
            herd's fears —
                        JOB,
the job's
        permanent
at ground level.

CHAPTER II

Centering as Transformation

THERE are two things which I have been thinking a lot about. One is the experience which in pottery we call Centering. And one is the experience which in nature we call Metamorphosis.

As human beings functioning as potters, we center ourselves and our clay. And we all know how necessary it is to be "on center" ourselves if we wish to bring our clay "into center" and not merely to agitate it or bully it. As organisms in the natural rhythms of birth, growth, and death, we experience metamorphosis throughout our lives, as our bodies grow and change from infancy to ripeness, as our capacities for inner experience enlarge and strengthen. As potters, we have an especially immediate and concrete daily experience of both these more-than-physical processes. For as potters we handle our medium in the full range of its transformations. We dig our clay out of its earth bed; or if we do not always dig it ourselves, we do know the experience of digging and preparing it. We experience the mud, we experience the forces of time and destiny that have trans-muted rock into plastic dust. We experience the raw ware, the sudden spell of a mobile act brought into stillness. The newly thrown or constructed pot has a quality which is not to be found in any other phase of its life. Part of our craft may be to perpetuate that "life" and feeling of plasticity in the rigid stone. We experience all the colors and textures of the raw ware and its decoration. The double life of color in pottery, unfired and fired. The biscuit, the glaze, the oxides. The transformations in the kiln during the firing which we follow through the peepholes, seeing in our imaginations the physical changes: the elimination

33

of chemical water, the clay "moving" into its stoneware form. The changing atmosphere in the kiln during the cooling period. That faint glow just before the darkness when we pull the damper out for the last drop in temperature. The fired pot. But even the fired pot stands in the long narrative of these transformations with only its own authenticity. For it too will disappear; it will be sold or given away. It will almost certainly be broken in time. The shards will then stand with their own special charm and symbolism. They may even be pounded up for grog and thus enter bodily into the process at another beginning point. Or they may be turned into mosaic for yet another experience of form.

And though shapes change, though each moment dies into the next, though no thing is being made to last, something is happening. Each moment bears life forward. It is as if the form that grows within our acts sheds each successive moment like a skin; it is as if the inner form which grows as a being within us is brought to maturity through the successive deaths of its material stages. It seems that the potter and his craft have had a special aura from the earliest times. Pottery is the ancient ur-craft, earth-derived, center-oriented, container for nourishment, water carrier. Experiences of centering and of personal metamorphosis grow within the craft.

Both of these experiences answer man's hunger for freedom — a state of being in which man's relatedness to life is unobstructed. Unobstructed either by concepts or by fear or by ignorance or by deformity. Freedom permits us to live into experience within and without. The outer shape of the clay is the extension of its center. We press out from the center and make the pot: the outside is the surface of the inside. We turn inward and outward with the same naturalness.

MAN IS HUNGRY. The baby is born hungry. He is born yowling. Hunger is a built-in signal. Man seeks throughout his life to satisfy it. Hunger for food, hunger for love, hunger for sexual satisfaction, hunger for money, hunger for power, hunger for truth, hunger for pleasure and approval. Man's hunger keeps him always turning outward, turning toward nature and other people. He gets plenty to eat, he gets a mate, he gets financial security and professional recognition. He has leisure to enjoy himself and to explore the world. Still his hunger recurs to tell him that his quest is not ended.

All his satisfactions represent attempts to gain his freedom. And the freedom he wants consists at one level in the capacity to experience in a living way a dialogue with the presence of life in which his own self-center spins. As he brings himself into center, he

34

brings into center all the knowledge and relatedness he has drawn from the larger life-presence that surrounds him. He finds that food, for example, is a sacrament of the dialogue between him and the plant and animal and mineral world. He finds that sexuality is a sacrament of the yielding of one center to another, the sacrament of love. He finds that his will expresses his impulse to give himself back to the world. If he is attentive, his hunger can teach him the interconnections of surrender and satisfaction and feeling.

Man has many hungers. But they all seem to me to be versions of a twofold one: hunger for freedom, and hunger for union, a dance of each individuality with the world.

Now of course these hungers can be sick, or "fallen" as the theologians say. And all of us are in varying degrees sick or fallen. But we aspire to being well. We aspire to redeeming our energies so that they serve our highest consciousness. And we redeem them, not by wrestling with them and managing them, for we have not the wisdom nor the strength to do that, but by letting the light to shine upon them. And where does this light come from? It seems to shine in all created things, but in our sickness we are often opaque to it. It is our task to make ourselves permeable to light by yielding ourselves up to it.

To yield means both to lose and to gain. See how the paradox is wisely caught in the words we use. I yield, and my being increases and takes form by having been given up in this way. Love becomes easier and more natural and steadier as over and over again I practice this act of yielding, from the secret inner center, the quiet will. As I open myself to the presence that faces me, it enters. It is a union. It is communion.

Freedom is presence, not absence. Centering is an act of bringing in, not of leaving out. It is brought about not by force but by coordinations. It is difficult if not impossible for a potter to force his clay into center simply by exerted pressure. In order to take its new shape, the clay has to move. It is therefore advisable technically to press down and in and then to squeeze up, holding the rising cone broad across the top, and then down again, one hand pressing the clay against the other. Tensions in the fingers, in the arms and back, holding the breath — these things count. The potter has to prepare his body as he does that of the clay. Because the wheel is center-oriented, the ball of clay will take a centered position naturally if we create the necessary support and influence. Once it has become centered, it will remain so unless there is a flaw in the clay or unless it is knocked off center by some outside force. The path to freedom is itself a series of transformations.

A capacity to yield is strengthened in the potter who does not merely use his material to certain ends, but who yields up his soul as well as his hands and his intelligence to his love of the clay. Once his soul is yielded up, the transformations of the clay will speak to him as his own. The inner laws of life will seem to be simultaneously unique centers spinning in continuous relation to each other. Peripheries will seem to breathe in and out like silken scarves. The art of the dancer in his nakedness and in his draperies suggests this self-indwelling and union of beings within the flesh. It is as if one could see how the life-body slips from the corpus; or how the body of another person's feelings and thoughts enters one's own, like lovers no longer truly separated by membrane or epidermis. It is a marriage of forces. It is a continuous dialogue.

We are transformed, not by adopting attitudes toward ourselves but by bringing into center all the elements of our sensations and our thinking and our emotions and our will: all the realities of our bodies and our souls. All the dark void in us of our undiscovered selves, all the small light of our discovered being. All the drive of our hungers, and our fairest and blackest dreams. All, all the elements come into center, into union with all other elements. And in such a state they become quite different in function than when they are separated and segregated and discriminated between or against. When we act out of an inner unity, when all of our selves is present in what we do, then we can be said to be "on center." Part of our skill as potters is to use all the clay on the wheel in any given form. Our wholeness as persons is expressed in using all of our selves in any given act. In this way the self integrates its capacities into a personal potency, as a being who serves life from his center at every instant. In this way knowledge can become a quality of consciousness and illumine our behavior spontaneously and truthfully. Personal transformation, or the art of becoming a human being, has a very special counterpart in the potter's craft.

One may think of metamorphosis as the principle by which creative energy is saved from being bound in static forms. Growth proceeds by metamorphosis. We can observe this in growing plants as well as in the world of men. From the seed grows a root, then a sprout; from the sprout, the seedling leaves; from the leaves, the stem; around the stem, the branches; at the top the flower; in the flower the seeds, the death of the plant, the seed falls to earth, then another root and sprout. We cannot say that the seed causes the growth, nor that the soil does. We can say that the potentialities for growth lie within the seed, in mysterious life forces, which, when properly fostered, take on certain forms, one form seeming to develop out of another, each needing that which went before in order that it may function at its own time and level in a total process which culminates in the production of another seed — that is to say, in a new life capacity, the future, the new unique being continually developing out of the changing forms of its nature, in time.

Growth in man is not merely the metamorphosis of his body from infancy to maturity, toward the development of physical seed. Growth is the metamorphosis of capacities; for in man there is a conscious being whose sense of himself bears witness to another dimension in which metamorphosis takes place. The physical man stands before us: a being whose inner experiences speak in a concrete if little understood dialogue with the tissues that bear them forth; the being evolves in his embodiment. Embodiment evolves in transformations of energy which are also little understood.

This is a clumsy way of saying what I mean. It is not a concept that I wish to convey. It is, rather, an experience of nature which I wish to summon into consciousness. It comes in like a light, clearing the mind. We want our minds to be clear — not so we can think clearly, but so we can be open in our perceptions.

It seems to me that the laws of physics are the laws of our nature, or else they are not laws at all. A physicist recently enumerated for me two laws which seem to be universal. The first is that any substance can be affected only by what it can produce. For example, in electricity, a stationary charge (or any electric charge) produces an electric field. Since it produces an electric field, it is also affected by an electric field. But a stationary charge does not produce a magnetic field and therefore is not and cannot be affected by a magnetic field. However, a moving charge produces not only an electric field due to the charge, but also a magnetic field due to the motion of the charge, and consequently it is affected by electric and magnetic fields. Any mass experiences a gravitational field for the simple reason that any mass produces a gravitational field. Since matter in any form is composed of mass and charge, we can see that any substance is susceptible only to what it is capable of radiating.

We can receive only what we already have! We can become only what we already are! We can learn only what we already know! It is a matter of realizing potentialities. It is not a matter of "adding to" but of "developing," of "evolving." We contain within ourselves a world of capacities, of possibilities, which the outer world summons forth, speaks to, releases. Perhaps this is why we learn most about ourselves through devotion to others; why we become joyful and active as we respond to the formative forces in the materials in our crafts: their potentialities call forth our own, and in the dialogue of which I have spoken, we discover our own inner vision by bodying them forth.

The second law is that anything left to itself will tend to equilibrium. (All chemical reactions are equilibrium reactions.) When man intervenes and disrupts the equilibrium, nature tends to restore it. But there is a limit beyond which restoration is not possible. In metals it is called "the elastic limit," beyond which the distortion is too great and the deformation is permanent. Any situation in a state of permanent distortion naturally tends toward disruption or rupture. For example, if one stresses a metal within the elastic limit, it will come back to its original state; beyond the elastic limit it will be permanently deformed and then rupture under a very slight additional force.

This law seems to me also clearly at work in a person's evolution toward wholeness. Even the body seems to operate under this law. Physiologists call it "homeostasis"; perhaps it is the body's natural centering process, a tendency that is always operative within it. On the other hand, substance is always "feeling" the pressures upon it, whether we are aware of them or not. In a condition of "fatigue," human beings like metals may break down under the effect of a slight but alternating stress. Our lives are literally at stake in the processes which I am discussing here. At each further stage of a person's knowledge and being, as each new step is taken, shifting the center now here now there, the tendency of life itself is continuously to seek a condition of balance.

As a dancer shifts his position he keeps his balance. He does this by taking his center with him, he shifts his center of gravity, re-establishing his equilibrium in the very instant that he has leapt. Otherwise he will fall and hurt himself.

The leaps we make in our lives are of many kinds. The point is that every move we make creates our destiny. In the wholeness of his nature, a man seems to center within himself, in a single fused presence, the mystery of his incarnation. Is this not the oneness that all our dualisms evolve toward? It is a state of consciousness in which we experience ourselves as beings alive invisible inaudible beyond definition, dancing and resonating and speaking and forming simultaneously in all the spheres of our substance.

Incarnation: bodying forth. Is this not our whole concern? The bodying forth of our *sense of life?* Is this not a sense fully as actual as our *sense of touch,* which quickens not only in our skin but in our hearts, when we say that we are "touched" by another's kindness? We body forth our ideals in personal acts, either alone or with others in society. We body forth felt experience in a poem's image and sound. We body forth our inner residence in the architecture of our homes and common buildings. We body forth our struggles and our revelations in the space of theatre. That is what form is: the bodying forth. The bodying forth of the living vessel in the shapes of clay.

The innerness of the so-called outer world is nowhere so evident as in the life of our body. The air we breathe one moment will be breathed by someone else the next and has been breathed by someone else before. We exist as respiring, pulsating organisms within a sea of life-serving beings. As we become able to hold this more and more steadily in our consciousness, we experience relatedness at an elemental level. We see that it is not a matter of trying to be related, but rather of living consciously into the actuality of being related. As we yield ourselves to the living presence of this relatedness, we find that life begins to possess an ease and a freedom and a naturalness that fill our hearts with joy. This does not mean that our troubles are over. It means that we are readier to live into and through our troubles, reaping their meaning. For I know of no trouble in life which does not stand as a counterpart to some positive capacity. Let us rejoice in our sufferings, knowing them to be symptoms of our potential health. Pain is a script, and as we learn to read it, we grow in self-knowledge.

The point is that relatedness does not end anywhere. Any state of being, physically manifested or supersensibly experienced, stands in a structural relationship to other states. By "structural relationship" I mean that formative sequences are at work in life, and if we could have insight into the processes of form, we would see continuously active metamorphosis. We would be able to see the transformations of energy, which are what I refer to as structural relationships. We would be better able to understand how organically our lives evolve.

If we surrender our consciousness to experience, our thoughts may then come directly from a living source, and our feelings also. I put it this way because thinking and feeling bear within themselves their opposites as do all other things. They may therefore bear life forward or obstruct it: the true face and the mirror. There are those thoughts which carry death by multiplying out of themselves, like cancerous cells, in a dementia of self-insistence. One may set off the next as mechanically as one billiard ball may slap another into motion. It makes a difference whether a thought takes its shape as a reaction, or whether it takes its shape out of a realm in which thoughts are the transformations of intuitive substance, into which psychic powers play. Our consciousness is filled by the experiences to which we yield it up. How important therefore are the disciplines which open us to life's stern and primal encounters. As I open, I prepare a place where the fountain may flow. Is this not what love is?

It is difficult to stand forth in one's growing, if one is not permitted to live through the stages of one's unripeness, clumsiness, unreadiness, as well as one's grace and aptitude. Love provides a continuous environment for the revelation of one's self, so that one can yield to life without fear and embarrassment. This is why love is in the strictest sense necessary. It must be present in order for life to happen freely. It is the other face of freedom. Freedom is the act of initiative by which a unique human will creates a new substance. Love is the experience of union.

The task of the teacher is to remove the obstacles that exist between a child and his free development. To prepare a child to take his freedom upon himself when he is a man. These obstacles are often physical, since fears or griefs that are locked in the body's organs will impair the adult's capacity to achieve the relationships he imagines for himself.

It is the teacher's responsibility to prepare the individual for experiences of relatedness. It does not mean distinterest on the teacher's part. For freedom does not mean freedom to have whatever relations you want; freedom means a capacity to be related to all things present.

Life is an art, and centering is a means. Art is a mode of being in which elements of form and content; style and meaning; feeling and rhythm — all the living perception may be imaged forth in a way that does not sacrifice the moving character of the world.

Every person is a special kind of artist and every activity is a special art. An artist creates out of the materials of the moment, never again to be duplicated. This is true of the painter, the musician, the dancer, the actor; the teacher; the scientist; the business man; the farmer — it is true of us all, whatever our work, that we are artists so long as we are alive to the concreteness of a moment and do not use it to some other purpose. Worshipers of happening, tender craftsmen in the full range and pull of substance, as faithful to God in the blown fuse and the disappointment and the difficulty as in the serene fulfillment.

The teacher works as an artist with the particular student or group, the particular situation, his own vision and his insight into the hungers of those in his charge. Every class becomes a composition, producing its unique revelation and tone. Simple or complex, harmonious or dissonant, galactic or linear, muted or brassy, teacher and students alike may awaken to the artistic processes at work.

We may develop a way of sensing each other, artistically, poetically. A person's smell, his hair, his skin, the tone of his voice, his teeth, his attitudes and gestures, his walk, the tempo of his breathing, his unspoken hungers, everything that emanates from him — all this emanation, as it were, bespeaks his wholeness: he breathing the world in and breathing it out again; a poetical understanding which we reap from experiencing each other in depth. This is not an act performed in the spirit of research, and may indeed occur from the briefest contact. A mere whiff. Sometimes one is unaccountably stirred by the presence of a person whom one hardly knows. But something knows something, that's certain. We give off, the poetic understanding takes in. It is a kind of knowledge that derives from the innerness of things. It is this innerness that kindles in the surfaces which so dazzle us. I find myself often in the plain gesture of shielding my eyes as I look into the glare of The Real Presence everywhere. One of the most stirring experiences of a teacher is to walk into a classroom for the first meeting and to sense within that room so much Life, so many hopes and fears and dreams and worldly innocencies. I bow my head before the power of the person. To speak to five or twenty or forty or two hundred persons with the continuous sensation of their unique individual realities humming like supersensible energy-systems in a room, with their lives at stake, shivers my timbers every time.

All the arts we practice are apprenticeship. The big art is our life. We must, as artists, perform the acts of life in alert relation to the materials present at any given instant. This is not a simple requirement. For each instant, as it ticks off, ticks off into the past; but the past is present in the forms we have taken. We stand between past and future, between the forces that have shaped us and those yet to lend their transforming powers to our growth. Eastern religions talk about karma — reaping what one has sown. We must think as well about transforming our karma through initiative. It is a matter for deep thought, to see wherein we are bound and wherein we are free. How best to grasp the paradoxes of obedience and originality. How best to educate our imagination, our initiative, and our will.

Moral initiative may be able to create an alternative to the death fantasy which seems to be a popular current mode of satisfying man's hunger for freedom. For the desire to kill and the desire to die are, I perceive, the other face of love. The other face of the hunger for union.

Death may tempt a hungry man, whom desperation has made stupid, with its false face of oblivion. We may think all our estrangements will be dissolved if we go back to the condition from which we emerged when we were born. But in our desperation and frustration, we forget that life is everywhere on the march, that time does not stand still, that the universe is evolving and men with it. We cannot go backward to a previous unconscious condition. We can go forward through the portal of Death, but we will step into that future carrying whatever spirit lives in us. This is what makes life so great: it is for keeps, it is on the level, absolutely serious. Everything we do makes a difference. Everything is important.

Since life is not dissolved by death, but again only changed in its form, how much more practical to heal the estrangements with all our present energy. (The Big Death is the Big Change: perhaps those who resort to it have lost all other resource; it is their desire for birth that compels them.)

If we look frankly about us, we can clearly see that there is no safety nor joy except in truth. And, as the most positivistic and pragmatic philosophers say, truth is what works. But surely nothing can be said to work which stands between a man and the fullness of his being.

Here the image of centering is useful. It is an act not of "sufficiency" but of "perfection." It calls upon an understanding of man's needs of every kind: physical, emotional, psychic, social, every need has its meaning in a man's life. Some needs are temporary and stand in the way of deeper needs. But we must honor all the needs as they arise and allow them to yield to ever deeper and more thorough fulfillments.

Art creates a bridge between being and embodiment. What are pigments and gestures, the ephemera of painting? Surely when we look at a painting, we are not seeing the paint merely. We are seeing something that is not there visibly, but which enters our perception through the eye. Paintings fade, peel, dirty, tear, rot. Pots break. Art in its material aspects is as impermanent as breath.

But meanwhile what has been its task? To perpetuate the supersensory awareness of man. To demonstrate over and over again how the joy of life is not locked within its tissues any more than the joy is locked within the smear of ink on a piece of Japanese paper. It somehow lives within it, and at the same time is freed by it. The power of a man's face, the supersensory impact of physiognomy, was somehow born into the world through Renaissance portraiture. The artists did not invent it; Rembrandt did not invent the faces he painted, he saw them. But they were there, and he was there. The artist in man performs this kind of function; he is geared somehow to stand at the frontier of perception, his soul pouring into his senses. As soul evolves, as times change, what he sees changes. He stands as a kind of prophet for his society. He sees space before science does. He hears simultaneity before technicians do. He experiences indeterminancy before theologians do.

Ordinary education and social training seem to impoverish the capacity for free initiative and artistic imagination. We talk independence, but we enact conformity. The hunger in many people for what is called self-expression is related to this unrealized intuitive resource. Brains are washed (when they are not clogged), wills are standardized, -that is to say immobilized. Someone within cries for help. There must be more to life than all these learned acts, all this highly conditioned consumption. A person wants to do something of his own, to feel his own being alive and unique. He wants out of bondage. He wants in to the promised land.

The artist and craftsman, however far he may be from an ultimate liberation, is continually willing his work. He devotes his life to acts which are a personal commitment to value. He is, to varying degrees, an example of a practicing initiative. A creative person. Initiating, enacting. Out of personal being. Using his lifetime to find his original face, to awaken his own voice, beyond all learning, habit, thought: to tap life at its source.

When the human community finally knows itself, it will discover that it lives at that center. Men will be artists and craftsmen in their life and labor. They will live as a community in moral autonomy, each man his own judge, with a minimum of external governing laws. The common laws will be found to operate within each man, so that when human beings become awake to their inner nature, they find that for the first time they

43

know their neighbors. Communitas is built into the spirit of men. They have but to perceive it to create it.

This kind of society, where individuals live together in mutual service and fellowship, and in independence, feeling the separation between individual and community transformed into an organism which functions as both, is the society which lives life as an art. Man as artist is on the move. He is not an institution, but a moving pillar of light.

When I was teaching at Black Mountain College, and trying to center the public-political and the private-human-moral-aesthetic meanings, I wrote a couple of poems which, I think, did bring together these realms which tend to fly apart, but which belong together. A man is a man, he stands in his privacy for all to see, then he is public. We shall bear public witness to the heart within. Everyman, taking hold of his life as an image of himself, shall seek to do this. If our hearts are flawed, the tenderer will be the bonds between us as we ask forgiveness of each other. The experiences of centering bring into joyful combination all inconsistencies, errors, and trepidation — all courage, conservation, and resource. It does not serve to count these elements as single and severed. They are transformed as by an inner metabolism into revealed person.

Poem

The way a man eats is political.
For political reasons is for human reasons, confidence vote is
    not entirely politic.
We fired a man from our faculty one year
And students of course asked why. For political reasons?
If for political reasons unfair.
If for political reasons then unjust, was it for political reasons.
Yes if politics are in the house, if they live across the cove then
    no.
No if politics is party, if the way a man governs himself
    yes only then.
I find it hard to answer honestly with care those who ask
is it for political reasons because I think about it differently:
I don't think politics when a man intimidates, I think human;

44

what he conceives politically grows face and hands,
image of government is self-portraiture.
I don't see departments, I see whole and I see features
some of them maybe political, pressing it outward.
Fruit grows on a tree, unless my eyes deceive me.
If I don't trust a man, his politics are not the cause,
Though they too stem from roots. So all I finally say is
Yes and no. And I find more and more that I say more and more
     yes and no
when I am asked if I think something is true, because
I don't think of what is true as any phrase one safely keeps.
I don't think ever so well-chosen words are likely to do the trick
or knowledge is now our homing-pigeon home.
I think of continually circling about and edging in,
But I wouldn't care much for a truth that was
"for political reasons." It would be smaller than a man.

Poem

Organization is not interesting, why.

If I am the chairman and you are on my committee it is not very interesting.

Or if you are the leader and we are your group and stay so who isn't bored.

Organization is all right while it is new until you throughly understand
what is expected of you and then what is expected of you
is soon no longer interesting.

It gets to be like a minuet or a masque that isn't play any longer but
the whole show.

Some people like to know what is expected of them and what
the consequences will be but not me.

Some like to set themselves goals and be clear about aims so that they can
formulate standards and have an institution to which they can feel they belong

45

But I don't want to belong to an institution.

Organization is not interesting but sometimes necessary to get things done
if there is something that simply must get done and better done wrong
than not done at all, are there such things maybe.

Governments are well organized but the people in the governments
do they see it all so clearly, who makes the policy and is he well organized
with the right leadership and support or is he a house divided.

Organizations and institutions and government are not interesting to me
and perhaps that's not important

But I see more and more people expecting from them whatever they are
benefits they would not expect from any of the men composing them,
I mean what rare bliss will organized humanity bestow that a man will
not give his brother.

When I was a child I liked to be a member of a gang and have a leader
and a code and meetings and by-laws and a constitution and a declared
purpose and a stern loyalty to our side. What was good was that this
public life instructed me privately in the possibilities of attitudes.
But as I grew and filled the rooms inside me I found the converse true
:   public life became a mirror. And so to play with governments
is to toy with mirrors rather than with men.

Will my bold anarchic dream come true and we will govern ourselves
unprofessionally, mirroring as universe our heart's terrain.
The private world is where men meet. It is much more interesting
not to say what you do not know, much more interesting to look
than to see what is not there.

Whatever has form is in the process still of being formed. Form is never fixed. Remember Shelley's "Ozymandias"; even the vasty monuments of those Egyptian monarchs

founder in the desert eventually. *Al wil passe,* chants Chaucer with good medieval realism. It's a pretty hoary cliché by now: how transient our world is and all that. Man's works decay. Man himself dies.

> Alexander died, Alexander was buried, Alexander returneth into dust; the dust is earth: of earth we make loam; and why of that loam whereto he was converted might they not stop a beer-barrel?
>
> Imperious Caesar, dead and turn'd to clay,
> Might stop a hole to keep the wind away:
> O, that that earth which kept the world in awe
> Should patch a wall t'expel the winter's flaw! —

mocks Hamlet;

> Your worm is your only emperor for diet: we fat all creatures else to fat us, and we fat ourselves for maggots: your fat king and your lean beggar is but variable service, — two dishes, but to one table: that's the end.
>
> *King.* Alas, alas!
> *Hamlet.* A man may fish with the worm that hath eat of a king, and eat of the fish that hath fed of that worm.
> *King.* What dost thou mean by this?
> *Hamlet.* Nothing but to show you how a king may go a progress through the guts of a beggar.

And so on. The earth has come into physical being; is eroding and reshaping continuously; will one day, we are assured, pass away. All forming, then, is transforming. But instead of experiencing this law of change with a certain pensive ruefulness as a sardonic triumph of man's absurdity or as what is sometimes called man's "tragedy," we can experience change as a positive, creative, future-serving process. Life is in motion — we are in motion — even the stones are in motion. So far, we have found no stopping point we can be sure of. Our pots are in motion. And our poems: no two readings alike, no two readers. And of course, most important, we ourselves are under way.

To commit ourselves to this process of transformation, firmly centered in an inner experience of law at work, is one kind of freedom. "In insecurity to dwell is Joy's insuring quality," sang Emily Dickinson. Life has an open end: surely this is where freedom resides. For there is no freedom in attachment. The objects of our attachment depart from us, or we from them. Life's impermanence commonly creates pain and anxiety, conscious or unconscious, for people tend to equate life with permanence. That is to say, if a thing is impermanent, it is subject to death. Death is the opposite of life, so 'tis said. Therefore a desire for permanence and a fear of death are related. It is my perception that a basic misunderstanding can be corrected here, again, by a process of centering, in which life permeates and therefore in a sense dissolves the concepts of permanence and impermanence. Life moves as naturally through the forms of death as through the forms of birth. The life is never severed, it is transformed from the shape and being of the flower to the shape and being of the seed. The life in the seed does not begin there, it has come into the seed from a pre-seed actuality.

But man is not a plant. And to speak of death as an aspect of the transformations which the living person undergoes is to speak radically. But everything I know about man or nature leads me to this understanding. And since centering is my basic discipline, I must bring everything I experience into the vision I project.

I offer this view of spiritual continuum and metamorphosis as an alternative to other solutions which characterize our society. For example, as I try to understand myself and the individuals whom I teach or my neighbors or society as a whole, I see many pictures of hostility and loneliness and boredom. As a person senses his life slipping by, the years slipping by and nothing done yet, his attachments may become angrier, more desperate, and lead him to destructive acts of various kinds, often against himself: not necessarily open, often repressed and disguised. Or he may be resigned and wittily cynical, as if fulfillment were not possible for man. As if man were, indeed, absurd. "The intolerable antilogy of making figments feel," as Thomas Hardy wrote: meaning, what a cheat to be given feelings which cannot possibly be satisfied. We are something between accidents and pawns in a meaningless kind of mischief perpetrated by heartless inhuman gods. What a romantic disaster! A regular cosmic soap opera! Poor Helen Trent, so lovely and so temporary!

For the most part, in our times, among the sophisticated and godless, I find either a kind of sentimentality, with man standing tragic and brave, under the cold stars, as they say. Or I find, in the more hip circles, a sort of fey and delirious relish of what is usually called "dissociation." The person dissociates himself from himself, and floats in a kind of deliberate schizophrenia, enjoying "himself," as if he could drink himself like a glass of water. A sort of inane hilarity breaks out in the gravest circumstances. Or a remarkable coolness refrigerates natural warmth. Everything seems self-conscious and calculated — decorative, you might say, even the spontaneity.

A third reaction to loss of equilibrium in our culture — an attempt to right the human being, as it were, in a centered position where his dreams and his practices may speak together in chorus — is the mystical intoxication of the so-called beat generation. These individuals look for ecstasy, for mystical orgy, for deity. They call their works "angelic ravings." Their publications issue calls for "life revelations." They are God-seekers hysterical with desire and with fear of frigidity. I think this may be why they rely on religious aphrodisiacs, drugs, and potions, to increase their potency for ecstasy and union. The atheism of our times wears the look of a religious fraternity, as it casts about for some symbol of union which all men may wear.

Dislike of death, dislike of God, dislike of soul seem to me to be three aspects of one condition; and its counterpart is the wish for death, the longing for revelation, and sexual fixation. Fear and desire are age-old counterparts. The fear of non-being, as psychologists sometimes generalize it, and the fear of meaninglessness, assail many people today; all affirmation, not to mention faith, appears to them to be delusion, deceit, a shabby act of self-deception in order to shim up one's shaky morale. Duplicity, hypocrisy, mistrust: these are the projections, by persons over whom presides the dual system of fear and desire.

Even the philosopher's reputation may rest upon his conviction that truth does not exist. It is somewhat doubtful whether the world exists, or I myself. The wound goes very deep indeed. A sense of wonder, of reverence, of mystery: an impulse to worship the presence of life in the universe, a sense of religion, is "explained" away as a need of man to invent something to cheer himself up. "God is a comedian whose audience is afraid to laugh."

Now this kind of cynicism, atheism, despair, affirms psychologically its opposite. And surely the muddle of our times is quite different from the muddle of other times. Our muddle about spirit in man and universe has been in the making for a few centuries only. It may be the price we have paid for our mastery, such as it is, over the physical world. In the history of consciousness, it seems as if man had to store away for awhile his sense of worth and meaning in order to cultivate those aptitudes for observation and measurement which have characterized scientific development. In order to develop certain mechanical abilities, he has had perhaps to neglect his spiritual intuitions. That is to say, he has had to change. And, changing, he has felt not at home, lost, "a stranger and afraid / In a world I never made."

But actually spirit in man has never withdrawn from him. If it sleeps, it needs but to be awakened. Man's awareness of nature and himself has scouted wide areas in recent centuries. The enmity between technology and human values seems a shallow war. As indeed most wars seem to be. The enemies are really friends, nay lovers. They need each other, can be whole only by each other's ministry. Humanists jeer at iceboxes, as if progress could in any meaningful way be material. Underprivileged persons jeer at democratic freedoms, as if free speech meant anything to a hungry man. But if we look closely at the whole picture, we see that technology has developed to fill a necessary role in worldwide economic and political change, which in turn is connected with new impulses in man's hunger for freedom and union, and that human values can infuse the machine if its role is wisely understood. This age has its positive contribution to make to man's evolution: an image of life in which man can center his machine, his work, and his values.

Deeply impelled toward evolving consciousness, men seem to be ever laboring to bring to birth in themselves new levels of being. The sense of peril is great, and indeed the risks are actual. Our efforts are our history, and our history may be read as symptoms of this work. We are in no way guaranteed our freedom. The body and soul suffer terrible strains, as the statistics of physical and mental breakdown show. We live within a presence which we may experience as a kind of inner lawfulness — a way, a path, which, if we hew to it, leads us into adventures beyond our imagining. If we do not hew to this path, if we are careless or proud and disregard symptoms of disobedience, we can hurt ourselves and others. Even disaster is meaningful; but its meaningfulness does not save it from happening, nor us from suffering.

The hunger in the present day for hallucinatory experience of a mystical kind is a true hunger of the soul. But although our vocabulary has no different word for spiritual vision and drug-produced vision, they differ, I do believe, in the quality of spirit present at the inception of the act. This is a physical difference and it produces physical consequences. For character moves within matter. Different bodies of energy live within man: motives, for example, are as substantial as muscles, though formed of different elements, and may indeed act within them. These "bodies" lie within each other, through each other, like transparencies, like currents of form suggested in certain paintings and photographs by movements of water and air, where it is possible to see through the overlying and interpenetrating systems because they are not opaque. In the material world of man's flesh and bones, transparency is more difficult, and only the seer, the man who sees clearly, the clairvoyant, can see through. An intimation of this capacity dwells perhaps within the recurring archetypal images of the crystalline body of redeemed man: an image recurring in the mystical tradition and in our own century in the surrealist imagery of André Breton's *les grands transparences.*

We do not take things at face value, but see working within physiognomy forms which may or may not be visible to the naked eye. In fact, more and more, matter is becoming invisible even to powerful magnifying glasses and telescopes, and may be known only through ideas, mathematical formulae; may be known, that is to say, only supersensibly. We are beginning to grasp the world as alive throughout, moving, forming, the divisions of language likewise working toward revelation. It is by now well known that syntax and vocabulary, the sounds of words, mirror the particular kind of consciousness developed in certain peoples. The study of linguistics as a grammar of comparative consciousness in the evolution of man, the roles different folk have played and are playing in the development of man's existence upon earth, is yet to be made, though many preparations are under way.

The fact I want to stress here is that one's inner life, one's spirit, is as specific, as palpable and material, as the shape of one's hair. The "I am" that one says to oneself is as concrete as the circulation of one's blood. Metabolism turns bread and wine into flesh and blood, and consciousness develops as flesh and blood die into it. It is a deep intuition we have, the intuition of the power and glory of death, the death wish. Just as love is a true wish: the wish to identify with, to consume (we consume our mothers, their bodies, their milk). When we separate from our mothers, we wish to be related to another, to consume, to unite. It is a fierce desire, the desire for union. At the instinctual level, we call it the sexual drive. But what does the sexual instinct mirror? The desire for a transcendent union. With whom do we so hunger to be united? The vagina and the penis hunger for one another, the mouth and breast hunger, the soul hungers for understanding, the body hungers for levitation, the spirit hungers for light. The whole body hungers for orgasm. Why? And why, at the same time, do we hunger for death? And fear it? What is the desire for un-consciousness, for sleep, the catatonic trance: for repose, for tranquillity, for nirvana? What is peace of mind? What is peace?

Just let me try to say how it seems to me:

The death instinct is the inversion of the transforming spirit-consciousness. It is only by death that we live into further consciousness, a state of our toal being which is present during sleep as well as waking. One knows that one grows by all the little deaths of flesh, the casting off of dead cells; one grows by all the deaths (the transformations) of feeling and understanding. One's babyhood dies into childhood; childhood dies into ado-lescence; adolescence dies into youth; youth dies into maturity; maturity dies into ripe-ness; ripeness dies into union with a world of being whose transforming dynamics await us.

Death and Eros. Working toward the same end. Evolution toward freedom and union. In our modern world there seems to be almost equal stress upon erotic license and destructive preparedness. Repressive bans have been lifted in many areas. Annihilation is an international fantasy.

Intimations of freedom are already active in the young child: in his hopeful face turned toward the adult. What does he want? Love? Food? A lollypop? Information? Per-mission to do what he likes without disapproval? What does the child want when he says, "I don't know what to do with myself"? Are these premonitory signs of the condition he will face when, like Dante, in the middle of his life he finds himself in a darkling wood astray?

How do we speak to the child's hunger? This is the question of the free school.

How do we speak to man's hunger? This is the question of the free conscience.

If the hunger is the hunger for union, what is to be done?

If the hunger is the hunger for freedom, what is to be done?

What do I do, when I can do whatever I want to do?

Fortunately, these are not questions which have to be answered by the mind, because there is that force working within us which carries us forward no matter how we spend our lives wondering how to spend our lives.

What we want is to be born, and to be born in the body. This is the instinct of our species. The metaphor of our animality. To be born. My hunger for freedom is my hunger for myself, for my creative initiative.

Perhaps this is what we do when we center; we bring the world into this womb-of-all, this central hearth where spirit-self glows.

Our desire to die teaches us to be born anew.

Our desire to love teaches us surrender.

Our studies of Eastern philosophy teach us to let go, to drop it. To surrender our attachments, our mentation. To free ourselves from ignorance and suffering. Our studies of Western philosophy teach us to surrender our minds to perception. Pure thinking has its source at the center. Thus Idealism is our Western knowledge: to surrender reflections for the evolving forms toward which matter is continuously casting itself, a dynamic thinking which generates rather than mirrors. And Western empiricism, which brings us back always sharply to the edges of a particular moment. There is only the moment, and yet the moment is always giving way to the next, so that there is not even Now, there is NOTHING. True, true. There is nothing, if that is the way to understanding how much there is.

Is this not the centering, to feel the ideal energy and thrust and equilibrium in the moment's concreteness? The centering experience is an experience in the soul, whether we get it primarily through hands or eyes or imagination, and this is its compelling strategy. When we are on center, we experience reality in depth rather than in partition.

Perhaps it seems odd to bring into center the poles of birth and death, but that is the poetry we live by. To yield at the center and to let another dwell there. In English poetry of former times, "to die" was a euphemism for sexual union: "I die in thee." Is there not this threefold wisdom of release, union, and renewal in the Liebestod myth, the Love-Death motif as Denis de Rougement has traced it for us in *Love in the Western World*? And is not this threefold image of death an image at the center of life, out of which new life is generated? Is this not a physics of the body, soul and spirit, a meta-physics? Let us keep to this radical physics.

Death as continuity. *Thou shalt not kill.* But unless the grain of corn be put into the earth to die, it will not live.

You can think of the deaths during a lifetime as loss. But this is a partial view. If you live into the experience deeply, you will perceive how what has taken place is not discontinuity but metamorphosis. This is a very important idea to meditate on: it helps to create a state of mind in which the meanings of history are much readier to one's understanding, and the meanings of good and evil, growth from child to man, evolution in all its markings. Unless we see and feel this continuity, it is difficult to perform the daily tasks of redemption, to love the daily toil and the minutiae of *scape,* whether landscape, seascape, or as Gerard Manley Hopkins put it, inscape. The disciplines of Zen Buddhism and Haiku poetry: the suchness of things. The horse pissing in his stall, the steam of winter. To inspire the awareness. Awareness in a condition of love. Love is a necessity, for life will not reveal its form to us without it. This too is physics.

But how are we to love when we are stiff and numb and disinterested? How are we to transform ourselves into limber and soft organisms lying open to the world at the quick? By what process and what agency do we perform the Great Work, transforming lowly materials into gold? Love, like its counterpart Death, is a yielding at the center. Not in the sentiment. Nor in the genitals. Look deep into my eyes and see the love-light. Figured forth in intelligent cooperation, sensitive congeniality, physical warmth. At the center the love must live.

One gives up all one has for this. This is the love that resides in the self, the self-love, out of which all love pours. The fountain, the source. At the center. One gives up all the treasured sorrow and self-mistrust, all the precious loathing and suspicion, all the secret triumphs of withdrawal. One bends in the wind. There are many disciplines that strengthen one's athleticism for love. It takes all one's strength. And yet it takes all one's weakness too. Sometimes it is only by having all one's so-called strength pulverized that one is weak enough, strong enough, to yield. It takes that power of nature in one which is neither strength nor weakness but closer perhaps to *virtu,* person, personalized energy. Do not speak about strength and weakness, manliness and womanliness, aggressiveness and submissiveness. Look at this flower. Look at this child. Look at this rock with lichen growing on it. Listen to this gull scream as he drops through the air to gobble the bread I throw and clumsily rights himself in the wind. Bear ye one another's burdens, the Lord said, and he was talking law.

Love is not a doctrine, Peace is not an international agreement. Love and Peace are beings who live as possibilities in us.

To love the crumbs on the carpet, the dog turd on the grass, the vomit on baby's bib, the snot on Johnny's sleeve, the stains on brother's pajamas, the lipstick on sister's pillow, tears everywhere, tears; and calluses. LOVE YOUR ENEMY, it is the only way to find him out.

Use your senses. Open your eyes, your ears, your smeller, your taste buds, your skin, your throat, your lungs, your heart, your blood, your interstices. Listen. If we listen, we will not have to ask. If we listen, we will find ourselves at the center of the entertainment.

Radio tubes are ringing it all in my ears.

Tune in on
NOTHING
astir with sound . . .
magnetizing particles . . .

FORM:

in a branch of electricity.

Contact with the sun
is about to be made.

If my ears can hear
the sound of the sun
I'll dress them
·by god
and put them on the mantelpiece.

Écoute — mes oreilles se dressent:
l'univers parle:
de l'amour?
de l'haïne?

Don't be idiotic — the universe speaks of itself.
We find we are its vocal chords
brushed by breath
speaking our own name.

LISTEN! DO YOU REALIZE WHO WE ARE?

55

Life always lies at some frontier, making sorties into the unknown. Its path leads always farther into truth. We cannot call it trackless waste, because as the path appears, it seems to have lain there awaiting our steps. We walk a magic carpet which, as we move, unrolls. Thus the surprises, thus the continuity.

In the centering consciousness I seek, Life and Death are more than friends. They are the mutual functions of a single being. A mathematics in which persons are not added together nor separated from one another; but in which there is an original whole, from which, through all the transformations of experience, one is never estranged. A love and centeredness underlying, which does not deteriorate as the daily shapes are "thrown." Separations continually heal and transform. Eros and Death, the experience of relationship and union in metamorphosis. Eros dwells in the body. Death moves through the body, an invisible presence. We cannot survive without it. Eros lives in the instant of bodying forth. Death lives in the instant of change. They are the bearers of life.

Centering as simultaneity. It comes close to the ear, to sound, everything at once.

It is a pulse, a plasticity. As you go out, you come in, you always come into center, bring the clay into center; you press down, squeeze up, press one hand into the other, bringing your material into center. Because we are working in a center-centered world, our maximum expansion and freedom is our maximum self-containment. Self-centeredness may be understood then in the sense of balance. We bring our self into a centering function, which brings it into union with all other elements. This is love. This is destruction of ego, in that its partialities are sacrificed to wholeness. Then the miracle happens: When on center, the self *feels* different: one feels warm, *on rayonne*, in touch, the power of life a substance like an air in which one lives and has one's being with all other things, drinking it in and giving it off, at the same time quiet and at rest within it.

This clay has a majesty which illumines our most timorous efforts. For this reason even our crude expressions have their charm and magic. We do not need to be free of error in order to be in the midst of poetry. There is a mercy here, and a transformation in which one shares. One's loyalty to one's first pots is inspired, perhaps, by this intuition.

CHAPTER III

Poetry

POETRY is an expression of the Centering Consciousness. By speaking figuratively, by calling things by names other than their own, it helps to enliven in us the awareness that all beings partake of each other. It is no respector of persons or of terms. It lives frankly in a world of shape-changers. For example, I go to my door in the early morning, open it and smell the air sweet off the grass and the garden, and smell at the same time the coffee steeping in the pitcher, and see lolloping down the road a young girl on her way to school, her hair flying, and at the same time feel the pang of young-girlness in my own heart and with that a feeling of love for the woman she will become and a love for what the woman loves in this day that is about to happen too. And all of this simultaneously, until breakfast and dawn and puberty and earth and the future and more all fuse, all center in one big breath of feelings and perceptions, and the will responds in an utterance:

> O the bonny cheer of an ancient day
> bacon-bright and coffee-thoughtful,
> I love its dawn and the dawn in me
> of my neighbor's child, when she comes lolloping
> down to her school-life and waiting soul,
> when I marry her!
> Today has its nose in her tattering hair;
> I'm pulled by the hand, we hug and we eat,
> and somehow the last love of our lives
> breaks fast here.

And so on.

I do not know what I will say until I begin to say it. I do not know what I have said until I begin to hear it. Is this poetry I have composed? It is a process of Centering which I undertook consciously at this moment of writing, committing myself to letting what was there happen. Is this what poetry is, letting what is there be there, radiantly, all of it?

When we become involved with "all of it," we are likely to get tuned in on hidden matters. We are likely to begin to hear things. We find that Sound is somehow deeply connected with Energy, with Form. Voice and Person; Form and the Ear. Recall the potter sitting with his head on one side, listening, as he threw the cylinder, filling it with air. "Music hath charms . . ." That's physiology! Its vibration enters our blood and influences the will in our movements. Even sounds we don't consciously hear affect us.

There is an ancient teaching that hearing existed before man was created. The ear is the archetype. "The ear is our mother; out of the ear we come." This strange saying is suggestive to one's sense of origin.

The other principle in poetry is image, or picture. This is carried by, or reflected by, light. Out of hearing and seeing, sound and light, grows our organ of poetic speech.

According to another ancient teaching, man has three ears: the outer organ, which bears the name "ear" but which does not hear anything; the inner ear, with all its intricate resonating devices, which connects with the brain and the rest of the body and tells us what sound the ether is carrying; and the whole man, from the top of his head to the soles of his feet and from his heart to his intellect, who "hears" the *meaning* of what the sound is saying.

It takes a golden ear to be empty enough of itself to hear clearly.

Listening requires a centering discipline if we are to understand each other. For what we say will be related to our past and future, to our health and mood and ambitions and self-image, our needs and our ideals, and what we say will be related also to forces which work in all men unconsciously; it will also be related to the weather, the season, to moonlight and the stars; it will be related to the history of man, to the history of the individual, to nature and evolution at every level; it will also be affected by the relationship between us. This is my view. Perception if it is true is direct: inclusive: poetic.

The poetic process of centering multiple responses in an organic unity may characterize widely the activities of life when they are filled with their total natural energy and will. When the sages of old used to say that poets are lawgivers, they did not mean that you could find legal advice in heroic couplets somewhere. I think they meant that the perceptions of the poets follow the natural laws of the universe as organism, and that to overlook the laws implicit in poetic perception is to risk estrangement from life. It is for this reason that we devote ourselves to a study of poetry, that we may sensitize ourselves to the wordless laws of being.

Poets are not the only poets. And poetry, if it is as deep a matter as I think it is, does not live in a house of words alone. If we wish to keep the law, we will look to the poetry. And where we do not find it, we will aspire to foster it. One way of fostering it is to foster in ourselves the disciplines of centering. As the old story goes that Martin Buber tells, it is not easy for man to stand firm before the fullness of creation. Therefore, oddly enough, the disciplines of life are those which create in us new capacities for organic response.

The sin against the Holy Spirit is the sin against new life, against self-emergence, against the Holy fecund innerness of each person. It can be committed quite as easily against oneself as against another. The Kingdom of Heaven will come when men are not afraid to be penetrated by bliss. It is a fact that the highest pleasures are the most excruciating to achieve because the body must be transformed, and this is painful in the simplest sense. Man has, oddly enough, to *learn* to be a naturally breathing, naturally dreaming, naturally hungering organism. It is difficult to be obedient to one's deepest hungers and intuitions. This is why I speak of Centering as a Discipline. And of Poetry as a Centering Process, bespeaking as it does, always, our intuitions of union.

Luckily or unluckily, the Devil is as real as his Brother, and may at any moment tempt us to abandon poetry for power. At any moment we may feel the tease of egotism toward disobedience. Suffering accompanies self-creation because the ego is entangled in the body and transformation of the one involves the other. The resurrection of the body may be understood in many different ways, and this is one of them: As egotism dies in it, as we learn to breathe right through the cramp in our jaw or back or stomach or arms or calves or eyes, right through the craving in our lungs, our circulation, our digestion, and out the other side, we find that our personality ceases to imprison us like a familiar and beloved tyrant, and we are free to live in ways we never thought possible.

The first birth, out of the mother's womb, is only a first. Those to follow, during the course of growth, are as specific. A man may, as he grows older, be born more and more into life, rather than feel it weaken and thin out. After all, a poem's end re-engages its beginning, ripens all that has stirred throughout, and engenders the fullest response.

The ordinary so-called science and so-called religion of our day, in the civilization of the West, tend to conduct a cold war of their own. They attempt to co-exist and to divide the world between them. There is palpable disunion. This split obstructs the poetic consciousness; it is a characteristic malady of our society. Warring impulses beset the personality: divisions and mutual suspicions grow as between one's inner sense of one's self and the social role one feels one is expected to play; between one's true feelings and social taboos; between the life that is offered and the life one wants; between the part of one which is unacceptable and what's left. The inner soul withdraws, goes underground, splits off from the part that keeps walking around. Vitality ebbs. Psychic disturbance is acute. Suicide may be attempted.

When a victim of this illness is fortunate enough to be healed, he is as it were reborn. For what were separated have undergone a metamorphosis into a new unity which allows the person to live as the person he is in society as it is. He finds a way to be a poet and a citizen. He finds a way to be himself and also the son of his parents. He finds a way to connect what lies within himself and what lies without. He has taken his devils in. Having become to some degree whole himself, he shows a tenderness toward others which is far different from the fear and contempt which characterized him formerly. At the same time, having experienced the consequences of his own sick sensitivity, he has a capacity to be resolute with the sensitivities of others. It seems to me that insight into the nature of schizophrenia can be extremely fruitful for an understanding of man in our times: both in his brilliance, his inventiveness and daemonic power, and in his warring nature, his drive to break through, even if he has to blow himself and his planet to bits to get there. He feels trapped and threatened by hostile powers. How is he to make peace with them? How is the metamorphosis to take place? Meanwhile he perfects a device which can produce heat beyond all fantasy: in this he plays with the idea of burning himself. For he knows that something must give way, some cold and fearful resistance must give way.

Perhaps the experiences of centering, however they come into him — through the crafts, through the arts, through revelation, through educated perception — will foster the metamorphosis so that it can take place organically from within. Perhaps at least if he feels that hope, if he serves that ideal, he will be provided with an alternative instrument.

For, it seems to me, man's destructive impulses are God-given. I guess I do see everything as God-given. Evil as well as good. In a certain sense man does have to "blast off" from his provincial self-obsession. He has to die to himself, in order to be born free in love and brotherhood. This is old stuff. But if it is the law, it is the law. And we may very well be seeing it take shape, in a distorted and ignorant way, in his obsession with weapons of destruction. The force driving man to transcend his limitations is compelling; his freedom to choose what form the change will take is in question. Necessity, and freedom. Freedom through necessity. He both wants release and fears it. Therefore if he can think of the release as merely technical, physical, "outside," he can have the delusion of giving up less. It is only life he is giving up, not really himself. He can keep his convictions, even though he lose his life. In this sense, it is always easier to die than to change; but, since change is the law, death takes it drastically out of our unwilling hands. If we thoroughly and courageously commit ourselves to the organic function of death, we will be able consciously to give up all that we have, "to die," and to let the new man be born.

A new age seems to be seeking birth. Much in the new birth will be rebirth of ancient vision; much will be still in the proportions of infancy. We are poems in the making: Logos at work.

The powers of man, far from being in competition, are the coordinations of his organism when it is in good health and working according to its natural rhythms. To accept the wisdom in all these powers is a first step, perhaps, toward their reintegration.

I said that experiences of centering, however they may come into a person's being — through the crafts, the arts, educated perception — may foster a healing of those inner divisions which set man at war with himself and therefore with others. A craftsman, for example, has the opportunity of acting out daily the wisdom of his organism, in its intuitive and other aspects. He has the opportunity to obey the poetic processes of fusing and unifying various elements in a single image. He knows that it can be done. He has experienced the mysterious powers of his material when he puts himself into a certain fruitful relation to it. He knows what can happen of itself once certain rhythms are set in motion. He knows that hand and head, heart and will, serve in a process and a wisdom greater than his own.

But more than this, the craftsman has the opportunity to extend, throughout all aspects of his life, the process and insights of his craft. Loving what is beautiful and useful and surprising, he will love the elements out of which the things are made: nature and man. Deeply experiencing the processes of his labor and his inspiration, he may deepen his perceptions of quality and relationship. Moral capacity may be thought of as the ability to be guided in one's behavior by the standards of quality to which one gives inner allegiance. Centering in the moral sphere enables one to extend one's commitment to quality from one point through all other points: to throw, as it were, a total shape. Craftsmen need the discipline of bringing into their thinking, their social deeds, their personal taste, their human relations, the sense of color and texture and plasticity and imagination they may mistakenly reserve for their art. To center is to behave as a person.

A growing poetic ambiguity in the meaning of "use" is as evident in the crafts as in education. The useful pot is looked at sculpturally, the sculptured form is used to lead perception forth. Conventionally round and hollow forms, or flat forms, are seen with more of the sculptor's joy, are less taken for granted as "merely" functional. A cup, a plate, a covered jar seem less and less prosaic. We have always admired in our museums the simple shapes of other cultures, and we are now more prepared to give honor to our own. At the same time, there is a trend toward a kind of natural bulk, crudeness, bigness — toward the massive and natural intricacies of boulders and canyons and eroded tablelands and stalagmites. Ash tray moves toward desert; mesa and cave move toward tile and bottle. The artist participates in a subtle dialogue with nature. Who is saying what to whom? If we allow our views of craft decorum to loosen, we may see more simply what is there. We do not need to fight for our right to be off center. We find that once we are on center, we may be off center as whole-heartedly as we like, for at that level there is no difference. At that level, we are free to create whatever form occurs.

We do not have to fight for our right to be useless. For we are able to see the usefulness of uselessness, and if we have fits of blindness, we have both nature and art to teach us that ambiguity. Likewise we assent to purposeless play, humbly filling our pitchers at its well, and if doubt and vainglory beset us, we may practice a humble scrutiny of the processes of invention. For since most of our living is unconscious, play is like matchstrokes in the void, bringing into light the structures we behave by, illuminating for us, however briefly, our deep meanings. How grateful we must be to art as it helps us to grow to the size of our reality. How grateful to all mysteries that lead us toward our clairvoyance. "O," as I once wrote in a poem called "By the Sea":

> O let's finish the song!
> die to the night's buzz! the peepering hush!
> Who's fooled by sleep? Awake we snore louder,
> awake we dream, wet bright and shrouded.

In other crafts as well — weaving and metalworking and stained glass and copper-enameling and woodworking and printmaking — the visions are limbering and expanding. The exchange between the crafts, the mergers and interpenetrations, are also witnesses to this centering attitude, which cuts across the lines and allows the values of color and shape and texture and innerness and architecture and use and inspiration all to blow like different currents of air into a single breath through whatever object we make. It is stimulating to work in a craft community where the different workshops are going simultaneously and craftsmen move with facility from one to another, adapting the skills of one or the materials of one to the processes of another. Preconceptions about what is and what is not possible are as dangerous in the crafts as they are in other areas of behavior. Meanwhile it is fun to play, and most discoveries are made by accident. A new impulse usually has to wait till our guard is down and our habitual views momentarily dimmed in order to break through into consciousness. It looks like an accident. Or an inspiration. But it is really an organic principle trying to find a soft spot to sprout in.

It takes a long time to learn that nothing is wasted. It takes a long time, and a lot of suffering usually, to understand that there is more to life and to poetry than our conscious purposes.

Language is alive in the center from which the poet draws. It has its bright blood and call still upon it. It has not become a symbol nor an abstraction nor a concept merely. It thrills in the breath like any tongue or banner. You cannot *feel* that life by thinking about it. You can feel it only by waking into it as into a dream. How alive a dream is! And yet how different from daily awakeness. To be a poet is to bring some of the sleep into the waking. To be a whole man is to let the poet live in oneself and to center the dreaming and the waking. Poetic consciousness lives in all our tissues, like a baby, who barely distinguishes between his joy and the breast that has given it. To live poetically is to experience as meaningful all that the organism is and does. To bring oneself thoroughly as Organism, as Self, into life and felt awareness.

In the middle ages a favorite literary form was the Debate Between Body and Soul: the material sense versus the mystical insight. Times have changed, and men have changed with them: now we are in a time of dialogue rather than debate. The voice of Spirit speaks within the experience of Body, the voice of Sense speaks the insights of Soul.

The disciplines of spirit are the disciplines of nature, which we come to understand through observation and study and which we re-create in our own natures. The discipline comes in when we have to pay attention to what we don't like, aren't interested in, don't understand, mistrust . . . , when we have to read the poetry of our enemies — within or without.

The forms we perceive through our senses bespeak invisible agencies. You may see a human figure before you, but you can only imagine Who is present. You may hear a voice, and in it, outlasting it, its meaning. Experience of the world is poetic, by, as it were, metaphor: symbols of a language few of us can clearly read. And yet, though I see through a glass but darkly, I am passionately committed to the figures I so dimly discern.

In the pottery I make, I move from the silhouette the surface the shape to the invisible space within, without which the pot would still be a lump of clay; as easily as I move from the membrane of my eye to the vision I have through it. Perhaps it is because of this fluidity, the plasticity of the world of forms, that the potter and his clay have so often been used to signify earthly creation. And poetic metaphor, calling one thing by the name of another: time an ocean, fog a cat, this face a garden, anguish a scorpion — seeing the similarity between things ordinarily thought to be different, the intuition of union, has been considered the highest gift.

It can all be discussed in terms of reading and writing. Or it can be discussed in terms of inner development. Poetry as Spiritual Discipline. There is a difference between what we understand (or *read*) and what we mean (or *write*). There is a difference between acceptance and initiative. They are counterparts, and interact in the health of the person as do other polarities that map our being: feminine and masculine, child and adult, birth and death. They are dynamics by which we live. Eliminate one, and the other fades. Paradox and metamorphosis are laws.

I shall urge poetry as an absolute and primal encounter to which we must devotedly surrender (as any loving Soul swoons terrified into the arms of its Beloved) . . . to images which baffle the analytic mind and yet bespeak transcendent unions; to rhythms that carry impulses of form into our being. Poems are structures by which we may stretch to life size: stretch our feelings, our perceptions, our intuitions, our sense of world as entity.

Man does enough different kinds of things, has enough contrary impulses, inner confusion, and general ambivalence to be a problem to himself. Either conscious or unconscious. It is the problem of feeling the whole in every part. It is the problem of experiencing himself as an invisible being, changing in appearance and character from age to age — an organism, a continuum, a person, moving from realm to realm. Pressures tend to make us feel divided among roles: domestic and professional, private and public, artist and thinker, the outward-turning and the inward-turning, live and dead. We must be poetic enough to give the lie to language and to feel the Person stand clear as the words change.

Differences join to make up the whole. As they join, new and unexpected forms evolve. An adventure in plasticity. Many problems can be tackled with this arithmetic, both within the individual and within the social group. In it, separations and disharmonies function organically, as by the tables of a mystical body. If we do not abandon the whole, if we do not lose the sense of organism, the more individualities and irrelevancies the better — the richer the ONE. As Swedenborg is said to have said, the more saints in heaven, the more space!

Centering the clay on the potter's wheel and then using it all to make whatever shape one makes; hearing the poem in the exactitude of its words and syllables and lines and in the economy of its total fusion — these are the same story. To bring universe into personal wholeness, to breathe in, to drink deep, to receive, to understand, to yield, to *read* life. AND to spend wholeness in act, to breathe out, to give, to mean, to say, to *write*, to *create* life. It is the rhythm of our metabolism and may not easily be put into words.

TO FEEL THE BEAT OF LANGUAGE AND THOUGHT AND FEELING AND PERCEPTION WORK IN US, PULSE, PERISTALSIS, RHYTHMIC PRESSURE AND ACCUMULATION OF MUSCULAR MOTION, WAVELIKE, STEADILY WORKING IN US, LEADING FORTH OUR ENERGY AND CONVERTING IT — CONVERTING, THAT IS TO SAY, OUR WILL. WE LIVE IN OUR BODIES. WE EMBODY SPIRIT IN ALL THE CELLS OF OUR BODIES, AWAKEN IT, LIVE IN THE FLOW OF CHANGE AND TURNING, AWAKE TO OUR ENERGY, AWAKE TO THE MOBILITY AND EVOLVING FORMS OF SPIRIT-SUBSTANCE.

This is high-flown and idle rhetoric unless we study to experience *in fact* the invisibilities of substance. We may become awakened to Word and what it is, to what the gestures of body-breath are which sound the vowels and consonants, to what we do when we *speak* to one another or *sing*. Perhaps Word is the magic stone. Lapis. The philosopher's stone, the transforming agent in a daily alchemy.

The sense of Word, the sense of Form, the sense of Breath, pneuma, spirit. It is like being rocked by the great sea herself, and all the waves traveling through us and making *us* resound, words ourselves, larynx, outcry, stillness which is itself audible to the clear-hearing ear. Do you know about the microphone which magnifies the sound of the voice box before the vibrations reach our lips? And the microphone that picks up the sound of wood and rock? Music is an element of nature; do we forget in what a mighty organism we share? Man listens to it as to a voice from inner-outer worlds. When we begin to understand how we are formed by sound and how we give off messages whether we speak or not, we will live each moment with a heightened sense of poetic privilege.

A discipline is a learning, and a disciple is a learner, one who follows a teaching. Spirit somehow presides through breath. *Spirare,* the Latin root, means *to breathe.* A spiritual discipline is a discipline of the breathing centers, which are life-centers. If we say that poetry is a spiritual discipline, we may as well say that poetry is a commitment to the Living Air: a faithfulness to breath, to Speech, to Logos, In the Beginning was the, to ... As a discipline, it requires an unflinching attention and a faithful care.

Poien, the Greek verb from which our word *poetry* comes, means *to make.* Poetry is making, poetry is creation. Poetry is the created presence. Word-poem is its echo, for poetry is the flow of genesis out of which poems are made. Poetry as an art trains us to experience what lies in the kingdoms of its origin and its consummation. If you think of Poetry as expressing undivided experience, if you think of Poetry as the organism's sensation of itself as manifold being, you will understand how it is possible to subsume the arts of consciousness within it; science itself. We speak of an act or an attitude or a thing as poetic when it includes feeling and insight and gesture which surprise us into a joyful discovery or rediscovery of Presence — which expand our consciousness.

If we think of Poetry in this root sense, we see that we are most poetic when we are most in tune with created Presence — person, place, thing. Which means that we may not divide life into the poem and the un-poem, but see that experience itself may be poetic. A little child who likes to make up poems knows this: that almost anything he says can be a poem if he says it in a certain spirit.

The artist, the philosopher, the scientist, the laborer, the craftsman, the homemaker, is a poet when he feels and tells through his being the whole story.

Poetry is probably the most plastic of all materials. Like the surface of water on which shadows play . . . What was that, dream or reality? a fish below or a gull above? Something stirred, a dark bolt, I am changed, how hawks rove my eyes and spill nets of fish too fast too fast, a shadow drops and gobbles the tears and I see, and I see . . .

The centering consciousness in poetry brings together those experiences and objects which appear separate, finding in the single moment of felt-perception a variety of elements simultaneously aglow. As language art, it occupies a realm where through the mysteries of speech, the multiple forms of perception fuse, transcending every single sense, and both space and time. In life, it is humankind's address: this flip from opposite to opposite, feeling in one pinch the Heads and Tails. We are involved organically in ambiguity, interpenetration, metaphor, and song.

Poem as visual object may use space sonorously. May manifest as theater of inner spell. Line length, capitals and spelling and punctuation, distribution of words, color, illumination, informal handwriting as well as printing and typing and formal calligraphy; everything that is visually involved with the experience the poem is celebrating may be included. Poems sprinkle down the page like soot or spilled type, poems are painted, are doodle sheets, are lithographs, are collage-drawings, are hand-worked banners, are visible language moving into meaning in cinematography (the moving hand writes, i.e. draws pictures; speaks, i.e. sounds).

67

I once wrote a poem consisting of only two words.

Hands

birds.

Two nouns, two sounds, with a long silence between. A long time of silence which is, on the page, a long space of emptiness.

Hands is an image. *Birds* is an image. Between them, a long wordless flight. Each reverberates in the stillness. The reverberations intermingle. In the center one begins to pick up the interacting waves of sound and picture. The winged limb at rest and at full stretch. Agility, grace, efficiency, versatility, the power of the small: man's hand; birds. How one may hold another hand in one's own, like a bird, warm soft and perishable, it is held in trust. How one may hold a bird in one's hand, and feel the tender beating savage presence; through all the tenderness one feels as well the predatory claw, the blast-off flight, the endurance, the skill.

One could muse forever on hand and bird, how they are similar and different. How they participate in the being of earth, both creatures of a feathered god with a thousand arms.

How hard it is to say anything about the poem without as it were putting handcuffs on the hands and tethers on the birds. If however one *utters the word* "hands" and then moves in its wake through the stirring stillness to "birds," and the two notes then work their magic simultaneously, the poem begins to live, and to do its work in the listening ear. There is really nothing to say, there is a mood in which quiet meditation seems most full of meaning.

Hands

birds.

Out of such a mood of speechlessness the poem was formed.

At the center of my thinking about poetry there has turned for many years this passage by Coleridge from his *Biographia Literaria:*

The poet, described in ideal perfection, brings the whole soul of man into activity, with the subordination of its faculties to each other according to their relative worth and dignity. He diffuses a tone and spirit of unity, that blends, and (as it were) *fuses*, each into each, by that synthetic and magical power, to which I would exclusively appropriate the name of Imagination. This power, first put in action by the will and understanding, and retained under their irremissive, though gentle and unnoticed, control, *laxis effertur habenis*, reveals itself in the balance or reconcilement of opposite or discordant qualities: of sameness, with difference; of the general with the concrete; the idea with the image; the individual with the representative; the sense of novelty and freshness with old and familiar objects; a more than usual state of emotion with more than usual order; judgment ever awake and steady self-possession with enthusiasm and feeling profound or vehement; and while it blends and harmonizes the natural and the artificial, still subordinates art to nature; the manner to the matter; and our admiration of the poet to our sympathy with the poetry.

The process which Coleridge defines has long been acknowledged by poets and students of poetry. I will discuss briefly its relation to centering, using as examples a few poems which will illustrate it at different levels of simplicity and subtlety.

Poetic consciousness tends to heal divisions between private and public, abnormal and normal, finding that the private world is where men meet. Because it is struck dumb, it speaks inopportunely. As we grow quiet, our love rises. We need only to get out of its way. Perhaps this "getting out of one's own way" is one version of the "actionless action" (*wu wei*) which the ancient Chinese sages teach.

Poem

Why is everything called
by another name:
water is smoky pearl this first bright morning of spring in the Mine-
      sceonga at a depth of 14 inches over granite
birds are flutes
grass is having its hair streaked
last week's sleds are beached in the field
it's all a big double-take, a dédoublement as the French say, a
      haunting:
the world is full of phantoms walking around in bodies.
The primal stuffing is leaking out all over the place,
it's bound to get mixed up either outside or inside man's speech.
What's the difference, the sages spend a lifetime trying to get to
      that supreme point where
everything is everything else, and here it is happening down here
      on my level.

It is really a matter of noticing things:

Imagine inventing yellow or moving
For the first time in a cherry curve.

70

"Why do you call it a poem?" my brother asked me. Well — because it is language, it is picture, it is sound, it is heightened awareness, it is feeling: it is composition. It has an element of unexpectedness at the same time that it seems convincing. It alters our consciousness. If we stop to wake up, we are astonished at what we perceive. Our world is a Wonderfair, and we are no mean attraction ourselves.

I have written several poems in which Man tends to be outsize; fabulous, earth-shaking, mythic. And in each one of them, some polarity is centered. In the following one, the poles of the far-away and the nearby spin an orb of feeling which travels in a continuum through both realms without being bound by either, like the earth through its Arcticas. The surface of the earth itself acts to transmit the presence of the beloved. The earth vibrates like a wire with his step, and sends the impulse directly into the body of the poet. It is the nature of the earth and of our dust to be in constant contact with the impulses of life. If we listen, we will hear the continuous tread of love, moving up our limbs like sap, like an electric current, impelling us as well to "stir and step out."

Poem

Picks it up, the earth, and gives it to me.
He somewhere walking
and the feel of it: like tides
fingering up, the feel
feeds up me, me a shore, a rising ground.

The earth runs round,
is endless.
Even oceans hold in its folding plan
and acres that sink
climb dry again.

(There's philosophy in it.)

No brinks. No
far forever lost and fallen away with you.
Bear up, I. Retaliate with love.
The earth's turned round like a mill,
and slaves. Observe:

We blind and touch-taught. I catch,
I catch your print, imprint, your pressing,
here. Up my trunk like sap — wells brilliantly —
my coils, current; nerve it is.
Quicker at least I am.

O it's he somewhere a-walking, dear.
You man and we can be.
It's the clay claims us and the
    day that says stir and step out
He'll hear

And what do we hear? For this moment, at least, we hear that the very clay that separates us joins us, acts as a medium of communication. Therefore the ordinary duality of separation and closeness is dissolved. Consciousness shifts to a center in which the polarities work like our two legs, bearing us forward. The left and the right go in the same direction. If I could have put this baffling matter plainly, I would have had no need of the poem.

Other elements too discipline the poetic excitement. For example, the ambiguity of "Quicker at least I am" plays on a double meaning of "quick": quick as meaning "living tissue" and "prompt discernment." "Quicker at least I am" meaning "I am more alive to the discernments of my flesh." Also the image of the earth as a mill turned by slaves who are blind, echoes the fate of Samson. And the ballad rhythm of "O it's he somewhere a-walking, dear" hopefully extends the lyricism of the poem's mood. Other rhythms in the poem vary from the plainspokenness of the parenthesis "(There's philosophy in it.)" to the syncopated Hopkinsesque alliteration of "your print, imprint, your pressing" et cetera. These ambiguities and reverberations are part of the meaning-music of poetry. One envisions the words spreading in clouds of audio-active spirit.

And another on that same theme.

GIANT

A giant lives in a house of stone
and fishes all day in the pool off his porch
for gimcracks.

He keeps a wife
who grows cabbages for his
springtime meal.

I found him out by swimming
up the creek
and hanging on his pole
in the shape of a toy balloon.

Granted.

He took me up and laughed
and blew me into shape,
face and figure female.

All right. It was all right.

When we walk over the hills
I swing on his hip
like a saber swings,

and when we lie drinking
under the waterfall
he ties flies around me.

I tell you this giant
and I
make castles when we want to
of jasper and pearl.
And we fill them with sights
anyone would want to see.

We stir the stars about at night
to soften our bed

and he can clear the whole husky universe
with the light he carries.

The whole thing is double talk — "sheer poetry," as they say, which means there's not a word of truth in it at the literal level. The sense of meaning is revved into a higher gear, an accelerated intensity, as if love had the power, once it touches a being, to reveal dimensions uniquely visible to the eye of the imagination. The imagination equips us to perceive reality when it is not fully materialized. The reality pictured in this poem may be thought of perhaps as the soul's experience of MAN-NESS, and of their worshipful play. The female is discovered into being by the giant, who catches her out of a stream and breathes into her so that she may be recognized to be the one she is. He himself has a wife who nourishes him out of the earth. One is reminded of the first two hexagrams in the *I Ching,* the ancient Chinese Book of Changes: Creativity (the heavens) and Receptivity (the earth); and the marriage between them which makes the world go round. There is a seriousness between male and female which we should not let our domesticities confuse us about. And there is a drasticness about contact which is innocent and terrible. It is an awesome fantasy to beguile a giant, to be beguiled, to find that Soul-Giant is Father-Mate, Lover-Brother, Son and Companion, no matter how life may seem to be outwardly arranged. Let me not think on't, as Hamlet was wont to cry. The very bloom and perfume of an infant's skin crawl with treachery and bliss. We swing at a mighty side; let us forgive each other our dreadful ignorance and childish pleasures. It is no simple pastoral, this simple pastoral of Giant and dame. It teases me out of thought, this birth on the Fishing Giant's pole, this pneumatic transformation, the energetic union "I swing on his hip like a saber swings," the embroidery of natural emblems "he ties flies around me," building with precious stones a visionary architecture, sleeping in the heavens, making space transparent.

When I am found by Love, I praise Him. When I am abandoned by Love, I grieve unbrokenly, bearing the pain of loss as within it the pain of recognition labors. For I know that Love is a power beyond my power, I move in and out of Love as in and out of sunlight; I pray for strength to go naked in His beams, for strength to maintain myself in the gloom of His absence, steadfast in my sense of His continuous Presence, no matter how or where He may reveal Himself. Love is Being, Love is Person. When I evoke Giant, a child speaks before the grandeur of a man. The powers of life seem extra-ordinary: magnificent, unearthly, and unheard-of, far more dangerous and certain than everyday grown-up conscience ordinarily allows, as it bustles with family affairs and occupation.

In the next poem, an effort is made to center the experience of loss. The beloved is treated as Eros himself, who has been frightened by his bride Psyche. In the old myth, he had forbidden her to look at him, and she was spying by the light of an oil lamp as he slept, when her shaking hand spilled hot wax which burned him. Eros awoke and fled. The loss of love through error is an insupportable agony, for one's heart is oppressed by the sick hope of finding all well again. The loss is somehow incredible, unthinkable, merciless. It is difficult to bring it into center. But bring it one must.

So the bereaved Psyche-Poet goes back to the place where Love had lain, and searches for traces of him. His presence is so strong still that she sees him everywhere, in the shapes and colors of the woods. And indeed he becomes a Presence inhabiting nature, both concealing and revealing himself. This transformation seems to make the loss even more cruel yet authoritative. The season is waning, the sun is descending into the earth, bright Love is a river flowing into darkness. Heartbroken, Psyche watches. How beautiful and deadly are the frost lines. How irrevocable is the future. Could one say that in this poem personal tragedy centers in an archetype? If springtime come, can death be far behind? We wind our shrouds like silkworms, we lie in bridal sepulchres, we do not know by whose will we are bound and unbound; for what spouse we ready ourselves.

As the river disappears, the soft mounds of its brown waves lift like rising bread. It is a moment of the tenderest loss and of prophecy.

THE LIGHT THIS LATE DAY CASTS

I sought for Love in the woods
where I had seen Him last

where in my trembling vision
He had awaked and fled

and now, in discouragement and grief,
I returned to search the place

drawn by a sense of infusion in the air
of that measureless union

pressed by a heart that swelled toward the pools
and hillsides of His visit.

75

To all the features of that space
I saw His face bequeathed: measuring
the atmosphere with summer's rapture
from within.

... sweeps His smile through the woods,
dashes light, the trickle of jet to the bright bomb,
mineral kings crowned colors of trees,
jade, agate, topaz, carnelian,
suspended cities, boardwalks, bridges,
mosaics and steppingstones dripped and flung,
visionary pueblos, flowering temples and pits,
a Presence
curls and floats and expires;
breathes through His pipe
warm music for life's slumbering oracles. Quick,
to the quick points the electric touch.

Truly, the farther into the woods I went,
the farther up the stream I climbed,
the more deeply I returned into His aura,
the more cleansed and naked ... —
the more His pulse and ardor built
until in the chaste and voluptuous brake
I fainted dead away, and fell,
a dead leaf in His invisible arms.

His Being humped in the stream:
He was a dragon frothing and dragging the stones,
and the stones ground their teeth in blessedness.

His brown transparent watery body
flowed and humped and rattled the stones,
and the aroma of the stream smote me anew.

I sat on a granite island and assumed His shape;
sloped over the rock, and the back of my legs an arch

of His trouble, my toes tracing themselves in Him
and He leapt up and batted miraculous crystals.

I walked tenderly at the edge of the stream
and my tears fell with yearning into the body of Love
and they disappeared, and appeared again between the lashes of the spray.

I searched everywhere with my soul and my gaze,
and I lifted my eyes over the earth nearby.
On a rock at the base of a bank, a handful of gold —
limp and almost drained of its matter — and I suffered anew.

The summer is dying, the autumn is clear,
the autumn is dying, the winter is in flakes,
fast into the heart of the earth where the sun descends
runs the river, the loaves of its brown body rise
in the light this late day casts.

"The First Morning" of any New World dawns in a world that is very old indeed. One holds within oneself, as at center on the potter's wheel, a single sense of maturity and innocence. In the archetypal Virgin-Whore, femininity is so ripened that any new experience of love rises out like a bud. To be able to be newly awakened! The new sun shines from its human stalk, the new soul swells upon his breast like a sweet fountain.

THE FIRST MORNING
The sun at the top of the hill
Fits its arm down my sleeve
And I run to you.

You pet me with your long light
And your white eyes dissolve into
Day.

Brightness falls through the air.
Where you are, dunes of gold
Tell the way.

Now sweeter than milk
On your breast I lie down,
A flower in your throat
My face to the sun.

There are plenty of things to notice, of course, besides the way love shapes things, reshapes things. I wrote the following poem after I had been struck by a scene in North Carolina in which a group of white student sun-bathers were observed by a black Negro girl passing by. The irony blinded me like a too bright light, as I saw those pale-faces trying to get black, and in their laws not letting that black face drink at their faucets. My entire feeling about the sun was affected. That's what I mean: you take it all in, the politics and the recreation and the social attitudes, the environment and spring. And human confusion and idiotic lack of perception contaminate the atmosphere. Prejudice and ignorance and fear eat out our bones, and the bones of our children. If there is eclipse at the center, everything is thrown into darkness. How can we keep our recreation and our politics and our philosophy separate? How can we not see what our eyes behold? As our perceptions become more and more coordinated, we grow in justice.

Poem

When the sun comes down to earth, so to speak,
we get into it.

When the sun lies long against the ground and gets warm into it
then we come out of the rooms and lie down,
bandaged here and there like warriors.
When the sun comes warm clear down to the ground
then we crawl on our bellies or backs or otherwise into it.
When it comes down hard
touching beyond equivocation
when it is not lost head-high in air
when the sun comes down hard enough to mean spring
then it invites us into it as it invites the leaf out of its dark twig
and pigment pleads its passion in the sun.

I know and reknow this every year.

But now I sing a different song of O for the summer color, for
seated against some sandy wall
fitting through rays, spitted in flame
captured by warm insistence and the
pleasure
of an even burning turning
darker
launched in light I looked, and found (struck sight) a black girl;
she swung her shining eyes
and irony spread in me like a natural blight.

Is it a standing joke for Negroes I have never heard,
what did Narcissa think when she passed by
and what am I to think when I
lie thoughtlessly turning black
in the summering sun.

You cannot catch the beetle bitter smack in the eyes
of Negros, I know,
you cannot dare the diffidence and their fear
nor fret to fracture the genteel plane they offer you
to chink their light and darkness through,
you won't live by this and like as well the good weather and the leaves.

And so we lose what I have always wanted
and felt close to in the spring. Don't talk to me about
the race problem:

To hate the sun

Once you begin to see and to hear, the life in language ignites, and almost anything can strike you as poetry. The sparks are released, the light shines, the word sounds.

To be a poet is to be stirred into utterance by the supersensory impact of sensory data.

so much depends
upon

a red wheel
barrow

glazed with rain
water

beside the white
chickens

as William Carlos Williams once put it.

Anything can be poetry that is felt as poetry. Some poets try to formulate the meanings they sense. Others try to convey the charge they feel in events by a language which keeps the power alive and the transfer of energy true. Other poets feel in language itself a special evocative power, and they utter vocabulary in a kind of incantatory trance. Language is mysterious, there's no doubt of it. The howl of the vowels, the squeaks and yawns and prissiness, the awful whirring and chattering of beaks; walls of consonants, housing those rousing vowels, shaping, dressing, flattening, catching, mounting, junking; the gestures of mouth and throat, the tonal form, as if man were the archetypal ideogram and language the vibration of his deeds. Poetry is immense, no matter how simple it may appear. There is no need for anyone to clomp around in big shoes and say what poetry is or isn't. First we must listen and ponder. Sometimes I think it is poetry if it resonates.

I try for that spring of life in the word. And I try for the sound of the syllable, the single vowel and consonant. I try to engage each free element in a whole which is scanned not by parts but from origin to finish, by process. And may I interject here that this is pedagogy as well: to engage each increase of knowledge in a whole which is understood not by single days or semesters or years, but all the way from birth to death. To keep primary our concern for the whole, rather than for special effects, however bright, here and there. Our delight in being dazzled or charmed is modest before the greater joy of being blessed. As Poet, as Pedagogue, I labor to rouse consciousness by requiring the most minute continuous attention to syntax (structure) and to prosody (sound).

Because language is alive, there is no mechanics by which it may be understood. We come to know it as we do a person. A person made it. And like a person, we know it to differing degrees in different circumstances. To come to know a poem more and more thoroughly. To feel it change, as we change. The transformations of poetry are organic.

Everything matters. The spelling, the position on the page, the typography; the beat of the breath, the division of syllables, loudness and softness, rhythm. All these elements of form, graphic and sonorous, help to depict the experience. They are the embodiment.

If we had as good noses or as good eyes or as good ears or as nimble tongues or as lively skin as other animals do, we would be better off. They can tell how we feel by the way we smell. They can tell where we are by the trembling of their skins. They can tell what we intend by the way we walk. They can see and hear into the soul.

Appreciating poetry is probably like appreciating anything else. It means having the generosity to let a thing be what it is, the patience to come to know it, a sense of the mystery in all living things, and a joy in new experience. "The simplest words, we do not know what they mean unless we love and aspire," Emerson said.

I have written poems all my life. (Words themselves feel like poems to me; and sounds turn into words.) And I think they come almost always out of a sudden simultaneous sense of impulses flowing together. This is pre-conscious; it happens, and then I am aware of it. It is carried by an image or a sound of words, like a magnetic attraction pulling at iron filings. Perhaps it is the *fusing* instinct, as Coleridge said. For example, I had been reading a book by Ernst Lehrs called *Man, or Matter*. In this book, there is a chapter on levity, a physical principle polar to gravity. Levity is the force that gets the apple up in the air in the first place; gravity is the force by which it drops down. Levity characterizes all the gases and growths which naturally move away from the earth rather than toward it. I found this an intriguing physics. At the same time I had been reading the Chinese Book of Changes, which has been traditionally consulted for oracular wisdom. It was early fall. Sunflowers were in bloom in my garden, their wide orange faces high in the air on spindly stems. It was the season of harvest, of withering. It was seed time. And there is no air so intoxicating as that season's. I opened my door one early morning and looked out. All the sunflowers were turned toward the rising sun. The sense of outburst in the air was unmistakable, at the same time a sense of distillation. The seeds had all formed and were about to go their ways from the mother plant. My heart was indescribably full of the simultaneous experience of dying and bearing forth, of levity, of the oracle's message of Decrease and Deliverance, of man's growth through time, and the ultimate release of his perfected powers through "death." And all because of those sunflowers!

LEVITY

Twelve sunflowers were in bloom this morning in my garden, eastbound

> brightly the animate disk lifts
> — the missionary tangle winds good up —
> in the soil, in the soul

> O
> this is
>   the finest
> w e a t h e r   w h e n
> gold dies, a finer alchemy,
> when gold's exchanged
>   for the dingy
> seeds (bed down, life is with us),
> when the sun grows old, the glitter congeals,
> the damp warm bright pulp into bits and tatters,
> paper and splinters and rayless wheels.

> this is the finest weather . . .
>   glass eye scantily opens a cold mirror,
>   shore winds, high tides of
> falling color, troughs and palisades,
> the gala inebriate storm . . .

>   (DECREASE and DELIVERANCE, how the oracle
>   speaks:
>   How days wane, the hallooing winter-ed solstice, the
>   hanging bough fallow, unflowering, less.
>   The increase of energy, the simple life, the
>   spending out
>   of spirit.
>   DELIVERANCE
>   DELIVERANCE

                    o my soul
                    o levity)

. . .   . . . the tide slipping,
                    arms full still of summer and
          the wine turns in your blood of dazzling daring dauntless dear
                    dear autumn.

          . . .

          when gold prepares for death,
          perfects its seed, readies its force
                    for
                              the plunge
          airborne, earthborn, readies the nut
                    for
                              the next cycle.

Sun lustre flower, bright animate disk,
          most radiant in power
to perfect its grain,
          how beautiful we are!
preparing for death
                    the living seed!

Infancy limbwise and full of will
          pulls us against gravity erect
tall grown in thought, in feeling bushed out,
the splendid bright face blooms . . .
          darkens, shrinks
and life in us toils
                    to die pregnant
(we cannot kill ourselves, we can only sleep)
          and
by levity,
          rise starward, planetary, off earth.

Look at this garden: what an august fire

                    circulates
                    to be thus
               entrusted   (thank you sun wheel
                              thank you seed flower
                                seminal geometry
                                    fiscal rose)
          and this man :
Look how gloriously we bloom
        en route :   the ovum charges, divides, extrudes, declares function,
                     declares heredity, hones its heavenly Excalibur on
                     the sands of time, in this house; brings
                     soul into being as sun is sucked out the green stalk
                     as the flower brings itself into being through the death of the
                     seed; we have no fathers and no mothers, are
                     not seedlings,
when, out of our brittle case we cast ourselves.

                         ⎧ the air
Look :   light :   ⎨ the harvest
                         ⎩ the spasm

     " — the missionary tangle winds good up — " has to do with that mixture of im-
pulses, creative and destructive, growth and change, which serves to perpetuate life in
the plant and in the person. "Missionary" suggests a purposeful tendency toward the
good; "tangle" suggests that the elements are not always clear; "winds good up" suggests
the spiraling structure of a plant form, also the spring-tension of energy movements, also
a kind of authority in the law of growth as we speak of "winding up" a discussion.
     The passage

               glass eye scantily opens a cold mirror,
               shore winds, high tides of
          falling color, troughs and palisades,
          the gala inebriate storm . . .

moves through images of autumn weather. The first suggests frost, ice, glacial temperatures, body contracting against winter's approach. Rising and falling, of forest as well as

of tides, are combined in "high tides of / falling color." By referring to the sea, it connects with "shore" and "storm" and perhaps suggests an immanent surrender of ego-consciousness. Again in "troughs and palisades" images of depth and height are fused: ditches and cliffs, absence and abundance, tunnels and piles. By "the gala inebriate storm" we are brought to the giddy drama of the forest when the leaves turn color and drop. It also brings us to the solstice, the period of hurricane.

At the end of the poem, I speak of man as if he were growing and blooming and bearing himself as a seed. "En route" echoes "on root." I speak of the ovum and its functions, and then I say that it "hones its heavenly Excalibur on / the sands of time, in this house." Excalibur was the name of King Arthur's magic sword. I am suggesting in this image how the egg is, as it were, armed with heavenly magic, which it sharpens to earthly use, on the sands of time, in this house; that is to say, in this body.

On one occasion when Christ was teaching and his mother and brothers were waiting to speak with him, he shocked everyone by asking, "Who is my mother? and who are my brethren?" Something of this sense of transcendent being is echoed in "we have no fathers and no mothers, are / not seedlings / when, out of our brittle case we cast ourselves." At the moment of release, each soul is manfully at stake — on his own, independent and buoyant. It takes courage, somehow, to do what comes naturally. It takes a man to become a man. And yet how effortless, how "light: the air, the harvest, the spasm."

The last poem I shall discuss combines likewise sense perception and reflection. On this occasion I had just finished reading Owen Barfield's *Poetic Diction*, for the third time. I was sailing by ferry from Havana to Key West. It was a brilliant morning on the sea. My imagination was hot with the beaches I had been wandering; my feelings were awash with the marina, ashout with Barfield's insights. He had stressed the originally metaphoric character of language. In the beginning, words are poetry, as perception is participation. Historically, language has moved toward prose, and the separations of "kinds" of meanings. Perception has tended to separate subject and object. As I rolled and mused on the deck of the ferry, the dialogue between nature and my spirit rattled through my notebook. An overpowering exultant sense of a primal union which Creation has divided: I felt my senses swim in nature's stream and my vocal chords speak with her wind. Suddenly Logos seemed fathomable: Word, and the forming function the ancients gave it. I heard the antiphony, or dialogue, of the closing lines: our voices give speech to nature, gaining from her their sound. Both may speak at once. The point is, the word is shared.

To OWEN BARFIELD: "Sea Speech . . . the gulf stream"

nature and spirit
the word incarnate

AI YA   AI YA   the green rigmarole, señor!
sea; wind; semaphore, of gulls. The
green
rag rustles, and abides. The
lime-lit decimal multiplies. REAP
the blue grain, DECANT:
decant th'Imperial flame.

I see that the sun is a red berry.

Oceans, of oceans, I
    cannot enumerate, nor re-
peat, measure nor cast, to count. Even
in this Caribbean crib, Nature you
are so busy. Changing everything.
Even here where it is still.

NATURE! her spittle, on the beach, her
salty tongue
                roping out rocks,
her edge —
            lessness, her
                        logos —
fleshed out: in, stands of sponges;
honeycombs for coral bees; gagging cranes;
whey at shallows; pelicans asprawl; . . .
her logos,
        is it meant to
                silence, us?

(white wands and streaming willows, catch syll-

86

ables; stone fret, hard and hollow towns
and towers — exultancy snaps
my bill! I fish, for words: still
screaming, die
                    in praise — "you
can't do better than that, amigo"
                                        [but
who's doing it — wait
! I've something to tell you . . .])   :

        the ocean's belly dance, its lover hovering horizonwide
        hangingfire shippingwater against her
        till flush he falls, and the dark, to lock
        in love, with light
        indistinguishable, the full dish of earth,
        the dawn of
                    a NEW
        day:
                    I give you the new born, the never yet, lived, the
                    not yet, dead, the
                    vocative 'declare yourself' DAY:
                                            NATURE, dearest,
        collaborator, the picture we make!: our
        son, shining, spills; He creates space; spurts, red;
        drills; and by our dance, keeps time
        ticking — hear the starboard swell click on th'hour,
        hear me trip, and reel, swinging my lariat:

Light makes Us one, oh MOTHER, SISTER, HUSBAND, VOID!
Voices, we marry, and unite.
                            Our light originates
in us.   See how we wave.
            See how
I am
            the thickening of light, its
trajectory . . .
                (how it escapes, like steam

                            8 7

See how you, Mother, nurse at my breast
See
        Our seed shapes
)
(ah
 antiphony, my voice
 without, your note's
               inaudible)

Because this poem is not simple, I will give a running gloss on the text, image by image, thus to elucidate the metaphors of nature, and the centering of outer and inner experience:

Ai ya   Ai ya   the green rigmarole, señor!

The poem begins with exclamation, utterance, *speech* — actually these are the sounds of a Spanish singer on shipboard, but as syllables useful in their ambiguity of sound and meaning — the green (sea green) mumbo jumbo, speech as speech, *une histoire,* señor!

sea; wind; semaphore, of gulls. The
green
rag rustles, and abides. The
lime-lit decimal multiplies. Reap
the blue grain, Decant:
decant th'Imperial flame.

"sea; wind; semaphore, of gulls" are language of the seascape. These are images of the "green rigmarole." The comma after "semaphore" allows it to be read fully as a metaphor before it is modified into an image of the scene . . . it is like striking a note strongly and then bringing it into a tone cluster. The "green rag," the fabric, of the sea rus-

88

I see that the sun is a red berry.

Oceans, of oceans, I
    cannot enumerate, nor re-
peat, measure nor cast, to count. Even
in this Caribbean crib, Nature you
are so busy. Changing everything.
Even here where it is still.

NATURE! her spittle, on the beach, her
salty tongue
                roping out rocks,
her edge —
          lessness, her
                logos —
fleshed out: in, stands of sponges;
honeycombs for coral bees; gagging cranes;
whey at shallows; pelicans asprawl; . . .
her logos,
        is it meant to
                silence, us?

tles, shimmering with audible life. It is always moving and yet always present. "The lime-lit" (associations of color, of theatre) "decimal multiples," that is to say, never come out even; there is always another decimal. Gather the harvest that lies there, blue (the sea is blue as well as green); gather the glory, the bath of the sun, as 'twere in a bottle.

This is another *kind* of image of the sun: its color, its nourishment, its everydayness.

I cannot state the immensity, the un*fathom*ability of the sea. New events ceaselessly come into being. Activity is dense even in the stillness.

The direct address: Nature! What follows is an exposition of nature's creative infinitude, her inventiveness, the creative power taking Form. When we contemplate her deeds, do we stand paralyzed with awe, unable to match her? Do I, as potter, stand hopeless with ecstasy before her stoneware?

(white wands and streaming willows, catch syllables; stone fret, hard and hollow towns
and towers! — exultancy snaps
my bill! I fish, for words: still
screaming, die
          in praise — "you
can't do better than that, amigo"
                        [but
who's doing it — wait
! I've something to tell you . . .])   :

the ocean's belly dance, its lover hovering horizonwide
hangingfire shippingwater against her
till flush he falls, and the dark, to lock
in love, with light,
indistinguishable, the full dish of earth,
the fruit in its orbit ripening
the dawn of
        a NEW
day:
    I give you the new born, the never yet, lived, the
    not yet, dead, the
    vocative 'declare yourself' DAY:
                    NATURE, dearest,
collaborator, the picture we make!: our
son, shining, spills; He creates space; spurts, red;
drills; and by our dance, keeps time
ticking — hear the starboard swell click on th'hour,
hear me trip, and reel, swinging my lariat!

The climax of my power is
to praise nature's hand.
You can't do better than she
does, that's certain.

And yet . . . Here the tran-
sition is made: there is
more to the story than Nature as a world outside us
which we perceive and
bless.

I begin again with the
scene. The sun sets; night
falls on the sea, locked in
love, in a way that makes
sea and sky indistinguishable, a full dish of earth.
Dawn is conceived, ripens.
Here it is! The New Day!

And this is what I really
have to tell you: these images of sea and sun and
speech arise out of a collaboration between Nature
and man. Our son (sun)
shines; creates space by
making it visible; spends
rays as a berry spurts juice;
marches in time over head
and under foot; Nature and

I (man) create time, I mark it by my swinging loop, my clock.

Light makes Us one, oh MOTHER, SISTER, HUSBAND, VOID! Voices, we marry, and unite.
                              Our light originates
in us. See how we wave.
        See how
I am
        the thickening of light, its
trajectory . . .
        (how it escapes, like steam
            See how you, Mother, nurse at my breast
        See
                Our seed shapes
)
(ah
    antiphony, my voice
    without, your note's
                    inaudible)

Light — of nature, of spirit — makes man and nature one. It is of our essence — we are light, matter, motion. The light escapes? like steam? (in death? to condense again?) Nature is born of man as well as creating with him new life.

Ah antiphony! Nature and man are the two parts of an antiphonal composition, neither of which can be heard without the other. Without my voice, nature's note is inaudible. Without nature's note, my voice is inaudible. Together we create each other — and the world.
                    Nature and spirit.
                    The word incarnate.

Poetry brings images of wholeness into consciousness, recombining what the rational principle has severed. But the severing has been meaningful, for by it we have discovered the parts and their architecture. When poetic cognition redelivers us into unity, it is the richer for our having now the powers of discriminated data and an aware self. A community of awakened men.

The discipline of poetry is both very broad and very strict. I listen to poem as I listen to wind. I study poem as I study cell structure. The discipline comes in casting ourselves in the forms of others.

Poems are forms of consciousness. We cast ourselves in the forms of the consciousness of others. We participate in the intentions of others. Whether we like to do so or not. This is the discipline. We are not always able to feel the love we would like to feel. But we may behave imaginatively: envisioning and eventually creating what is not yet present. This is what I call Moral Imagination. The disciplines of poetry are related to the development of this faculty.

We commit ourselves to the discipline of poetry *not* in order to understand the poet's point of view nor to delight in his music. These are pleasures, but they are not primary. We commit ourselves to participation, and poetry is a means. Poetic form, which is in fact poetic music, delivers us into a common measure. We cannot remain separate from the poem if we sing it.

But another step awaits us. Now it is our turn to speak. What do we say?

If we don't see all the meanings clearly, that's to be expected. If we have to study long to grasp how life moves by a dynamic of interacting opposites, how the future streams toward us transforming our bodies and our spirits, how the present streams away into the past and plays back into our future, how deep and unapparent the appearances of good and evil are . . . if we have to study long to discover what we have to say, that's not surprising.

But we do ourselves a disservice if we believe the sources of speech are conscious — if we believe that because we cannot think of anything to say, we do indeed have nothing to say. It is useful to distinguish between two modes of utterance: speech and song.

Speech, broadly understood, occurs in a spirit of dialogue. We learn to speak by hearing the speech around us. We respond.

Song is self-generated, may indeed be wordless, is the utterance of the soul in its living and sounding forth, is the ecstatic cry of one's sense of Self. Another may hear our song and be stirred. Or we may hear his song and be stirred. Yet singing to oneself has another quality than talking to oneself.

What we have to say, then, may be neither pure speech nor pure song, but some moment in their intersection.

We listen. We envision. We open our mouths and out it comes. It is difficult to be as simple as we are, and as natural, and as beautiful. We are oppressed and inhibited by concepts which are Luciferic in their pride and in their disobedience. They are temptations. We may, for example, be tempted to think that when we speak, we must say something intelligent and worth hearing. But we don't really know what intelligence is. Nor may we easily judge worth. If we would speak simply to one another, sincerely, in our most natural human concern, with body warmth — if we say "hello" in such a spirit, what could be more poetic or wiser or more dazzling?

Someone once asked me what a poet does, how a poet works. Does he hear voices?

I have pondered this question, and I have come to think that "voices" are a late stage in the poetic process, after the transformation of experience into words has already begun. By the time the inner voices speak, the poem is already beyond genesis and the first metamorphosis; it is already language and image. The unconscious "ear" hears ahead of the conscious hand. As the poet begins, the composition is already so far advanced at the unconscious level that words are forming, and he does, as it were, listen. A line comes to him.

Perhaps it goes something like this: The poet has an experience of meaning. He feels himself drawn in a kind of spiritual traffic; sensations of energy and excitement course through him like new life; sensations of import are unmistakable; the value is the response that is taking place in him organically; it is his nature to respond more than ordinary men do. "Awe before the pure phenomenon," as Goethe said.

Out of this spiritual traffic is born the poem through the channel of breath, the *spiritus* of the poet. It is both his and not his; any mother would say the same of her child. Without him it would not exist. If it were up to him alone, it would not exist. It is a communication. Those who have ears to hear, let them hear. The experience flows like a charge into the organism. It spreads, it stirs, it breeds sound and picture, it warms and enlightens.

Say the poet does make contact with meaning at this deep level, becomes charged with it; he rarely does so abstractly. Often the converter is a sensation of some kind: a word, person, place, dream, event, movement. This image acts as a communication center, receiving and sending messages, accumulating information. These messages are impulses, not yet words. The impulses travel in waves of light and sound. Out of these perhaps language develops. The mystery is partly that the poetry lies elsewhere, lies un-speakable and permeating; and this is the poetry that the poet's body absorbs. Truth be-comes part of him, and in his breath takes shape as speech. The element that assures the poetry and does not allow it to die into content is the alchemy of its sound.

The artist, the poet, the maker, the true scientist, works from inspiration. What now comes to us as inspiration, so that we commonly refer to the "mysterious" processes of creation, may one day lie open to consciousness. The experience of art may train in us faculties for higher perception. Music helps to open our ears in the most ultimate sense and to bring them into function as organs of form. Poetry helps us to see in a single vision the physical systems of light and sound, and to experience as One Bath the thousand prisms of a lively shower. If our destiny as human beings is not to amass wealth and in-fluence, but to perfect ourselves, then the artist too is such a being. It seems as if often his ordeal is the greater, to take his gifts with him when he leaves his studio. Otherwise he may seem to be engaged not with manhood but with a trade. Here the importance of cen-tering seems emphatic.

For there is something, you see, that I am interested in: something that is served by poetry, by pottery, by daily deed of imagination and the conscious experiences of forming — something that is served by Art. For Art, no matter how high its mission, serves in yet a higher. It is a bridge between the visible and invisible worlds. No one would think for a moment that the power of the Mona Lisa consists of the aging paint on the deteriorating canvas. Who is smiling through the rags and tatters of perpetually decaying matter?

Artistic vision registers and prophesies the expanding consciousness of man. I am not speaking only of works of art, but of artistic vision wherever it imbues living acts. Ar-tistic imagination creates what has never before existed. To live artistically is to embody in social forms the unique individual and the intuitions of union.

In the prophetic artist, genesis again will create the firmament and the day and night and the world of plants and animals, and into this creation he will enter and he will be its voice and its guardian and will give to everything its name which is poetry and to every-thing its sound which is music and to everything its color which is painting and to every-thing its shape which is architecture and to everything its motion which is dance and to everything its metamorphosis which is sculpture. He will not be a spectator, enchanted by cinders and agony, observing his desires with the detachment of a spellbound anchorite delirious in the desert. Nor will he play with the unknown as with a toy that has no menace in it. In deepest commitment to the possibilities of creation, he will pour the spirit of art into works of life.

Poetic images create in us capacities for personal reality and for participation. They are the joyful breathing at our source.

CHAPTER IV

Pedagogy

"ALL writing is swinishness. People who emerge from vagueness to try to state precisely anything that is going on in their minds are swine. The entire literary tribe is swinish, especially today. All those who have mental landscapes — I mean in certain parts of their minds, of their heads — in well-defined areas of their brains; all who are masters of their language, those for whom words have a meaning, all those for whom the soul has its heights and thought its currents, those who are the spirit of the epoch, and who have given names to these currents of thought — I am thinking of the special joy of each one and of the robot-like creaking they produce, at every gust of wind — all of them are swine."

So wrote Antonin Artaud. This is strong language. I quote it because it is strong. And I quote it in order to remind myself and my reader that, for all my conscientious efforts here to write down my thoughts about matters of true concern to me, there is a world of difference between these sentences and the experiences to which they refer. I feel this difference nowhere more strongly than when I am talking about teaching.

It is possible in life to be many things at once. It is hard to say everything at once. We play upon the ambiguities of words as deftly as we can, and yet we are not sure how successfully we have kept paradox alive in their ring. Life is bipolar. Everything contains its opposite. OK. So when I say "teacher," remember that I mean "non-teacher." When I say "person," remember that I mean "student." Remember that all the time I am talking, I am talking about life, no matter what I may seem to be saying. Try to hear the whole reverberating through the parts. Experience is education. What I say about Pedagogy applies to both the profession of teaching and the non-profession of manhood. We teach all the time, by what we are and what we do. We learn all the time, by what we see and feel and think and do. The capacity to learn and to teach is organic. We take in and we give out. Every breath changes us. Metamorphosis occurs at every level. And yet the more we learn and change, the more revealed we stand.

There is a difference, then, between what dies in change and what continues to grow, ever riper, ever more complete. Forms fall away in order that form may be revealed. There must therefore be aspects of our physiques which function on behalf of death, and aspects which function on behalf of continuum. I think it is a mistake to lump everything together and say that because one element behaves in a certain way, every other element behaves in that way; to say that because flesh rots, souls do. I see that the mineral body decays. And I see that there are relationships between its decay and the development of inner maturity. Death begins at birth, and so does growth. The "body" or "form" that matures is literally not the same as that which perishes.

The American Dream wants a beautiful body. And some of its intellectual and spiritual leadership is discussing drugs as doorways to mystical consciousness. Thus is man's ancient hunger for physical perfection and transcendent vision popularly reflected. The fusion of these images of beauty and truth has appeared in mystical tradition as embodied ecstasy. A resurrected body may be this one, whose physicality transcends the limitations of matter as they now appear to us. Perhaps this will be the new Adam. Perhaps the lifelong efforts of our pedagogy to bring us into center, open and ready and resilient and in tune with the various spheres of our universe, bear us toward this gracious vision.

Pedagogy is a formidable name for a simple act. It comes from two Greek words, meaning *child* and *to lead*. A pedagogue is one who leads a child, and pedagogy is his craft as teacher. *Education* is an interesting word too, for it also comes from two other words — in Latin — meaning *out* and *to draw* or *to lead*. To educate is to *draw out*, to *lead out*. In some sense, then, we must be *in*!

Where is it we want to go? The question of pedagogy is the question of man's destiny. It is the question of Person. My friends tell me that they have plenty to do just living their daily lives and doing their work without worrying about human destiny! OK. But daily life reverberates with metaphors. The daily act of centering clay on the potter's wheel opens a world of meanings. Or someone comes to the door and says Hello and one feels in the presence of poetry. Wordsworth felt that supercharge in the ordinary incidents of life. "To me the meanest flower that blows can give / Thoughts that do often lie too deep for tears." And Gerard Manley Hopkins for whom "all trades, their gear and tackle and trim" were "news of God." And the Japanese poets of haiku and senryu, the celebrants supremely of "occasions." These poetic spirits are part of a fellowship remarking revelation in the everyday.

Whether or not we face the question of pedagogy consciously, we are answering it, for our actions speak no matter what our lips do or do not say. Responses are values, and the responses we foster are the values we teach. There ain't no hidin' place down here; we color the atmosphere by our presence in it.

I said earlier that I could not talk about the handcrafts without talking about the spirit of man. I cannot speak about pedagogy without speaking about spiritual growth. Whether one is teaching poetry or pottery, writing or sculpture, one is teaching metaphysics. As I urge upon my students the psychic and muscular coordinations of form and the revelry of dissociation, I feel myself hopping with glee, as if we were all being stirred by a mighty spoon. To be baked as a loaf, to be eaten by a god-mouth, to turn into divinity . . . What is that sweet smell in the air as we labor together?

Life in the classroom is real, adventuresome, thrilling, and demanding. How do we get ourselves out in the open? How do we wake up? We are always working to rouse our sleeping organs and to bring our waking ones into prime functioning. It is like discovering the world each time we meet. I once wrote a poem about it. I wrote it at a time in my life when I was in great emotional trouble; and when I am in trouble inwardly, my reflex is to contract away from the world, to withdraw, to become immobile. I have to work very hard to counteract this tendency in myself and to turn the tide, as you might say, when the pulling away begins. So one wintry evening I was sitting in my farmhouse looking out the window at an evergreen tree and meditating on difficulties I faced owing to my character and circumstances. I began to write down my thoughts. The act of writing limbered my dragging heart and enlivened my perceptions. My thoughts began to pull from inside outward. As the form of my concentration expanded, taking in more and more of the actualities of my life, including my job as teacher, other feelings began to swell. I believe there is a potter's truth here: If I begin at the center, firmly and gently, and if I open my clay firmly and gently, pulling the walls out from the center, opening wider and wider, as wide as the clay will allow, this crescent will form within me like a grace. If I make this act gently and firmly and unselfconsciously, like a craftsman ably handling his material, I will make something useful and beautiful. It does not take long to do if you know what you are doing. But some of us have to serve a lengthy apprenticeship.

Poem

TO MY CLASS

I am sixty-five years old and have no wisdom.
I love you all, each one of you. Crushed
in a shining room, your sweet sap runs,
berries goldenrod flesh and the flowing eyes,
flush my face with their radiant spray, drink
is the course it takes. I reel in the brimful sep-
ulchre.
       To be so devastated at your taste, the single
joy each one of you declares in me. Thou, my self, come
to the gate of sense and soul a tidal cup,
I dash you to the wall of the world, spill you green
to its halls, every other man I know shines
with your wetness like pebbles more themselves
in the sea, spirits drunk.
       I owe you life.

I am a teacher, and therefore I am interested in search and growth, schools and methods. Or does it work the other way round? In education as in handcraft, I am interested in questions of meaning and technique. Since teaching and learning cannot be avoided, what can we contribute to the natural process? What kind of environment and inner activity take us toward rebirth rather than toward perpetuation? How to teach Reading and Writing? Self-reliance and Community? Art? And what about textbooks?

My search has been for an impulse in education which may bring together the full range of human capacity and knowledge, the full figure of historical man, of prophetic man; earth; cosmos; the whole story. Every step I take brings me closer to where I am.

The questions I have raised about my own life and education have led me gradually to children. I am looking for a pedagogical understanding of man from infancy to age. It is part of a centering process which seeks to bring into wholeness a picture of Person.

I want to know why a child is sent to school at all. Why at one age rather than another. Why he is taught one subject now and another later on. And I don't want to be told that it is to keep up with an enemy or that it is legally required or that it's what an expert recommends. I want to know how it gets that way, in the enemy's or law's or expert's mind. I am not satisfied with opportunism or experiment as a rationale of curriculum. I want to know what needs (whose needs) are being served by doing things one way rather than another, and what makes anybody think so. I want to know what happens to the artist who lives naturally in a child's responsiveness to rhythm and tone and color and story, what happens to the child in man. I want to know why so many grown-ups who are smart in school blow their brains out in middle age, or rely on anxiety depressants. I want the whole story from beginning to end. There are answers to these questions.

I have come during the period of my researches to a characteristic intersection of attitudes toward the education of children: the new Rousseauism of A. S. Neill's theory of the free child, and the new Goetheanism of Rudolph Steiner's pedagogy based upon the metamorphosis of capacities (which may lead eventually to freedom from habit and unconsciousness). I say "characteristic intersection" because I think these two men express a polarity basic to our time. Neill's school, Summerhill, arose as a reaction against the repressive culture of Victorian England and as an expression of Neill's psychological insights into childhood guilt and sexuality. His intuitions seem to me to work between societal influences and individual freedom from those influences. Societal influence is often repressive, and therefore the spirit of Summerhill is reactive. Since freedom is conceived as freedom from societal pressure, it is clearer what Summerhill is *against* than what it is for. But this is a real position, and we must indeed sharpen our resistances to useless knowledge, lies, unjust laws, compulsion, mechanical procedure, and fear of libidinal fire. Society within Summerhill is the company of children and teachers, who meet together to govern their affairs in common. The child is at the enter of Neill's concern.

What is a child? Who is this child? Who may he become? These are Rudolph Steiner's questions. His intuitions seem to me to move between archetype and individual; and the processes of growth as he indicates them are not either reactive nor spontaneous, but organic. Free will is not against, but *on behalf of*. When a young man, Steiner was asked to edit the scientific writing of Goethe for the Weimar edition. Goethe's concept of metamorphosis became the root from which Steiner's pedagogy unfolded. In 1919, he was asked to create a school for the children of factory workers in Stuttgart. This was the first Waldorf School. There are now more than sixty in more than thirty countries. Special work is done with handicapped persons. It is the closest thing I have found to a centering impulse in education.

Rudolph Steiner's mind was open to the most difficult questions, and he was prepared to go very far indeed to listen for answers. He perceived man as both historical and prophetic, standing between the effects of the past and the instreaming of the future, an evolving organism of body, soul, and spirit; part of a vast world of being, in which the earth and the sphere it inhabits are likewise an evolving organism.

This sense of organism was embodied then in an educational method. The rhythms of that education are the long rhythms of our growth, inner changes corresponding to the physical changes of the developing body. Curriculum becomes the image of the metamorphosis of man's capacities. Since everything is part of an organism, everything is related. An anatomy of relationships is part of Steiner's contribution. These relationships are kept alive in the methods of teaching he suggests.

The teacher handles the living and growing child with the same sense of immediacy and particularity and beauty that the artist experiences in relation to his materials and vision. The teacher works in a certain state of mind, with certain knowledge and aims, primarily listening to what the child is telling him through its body and its behavior and its fantasies and its play and speech. He does not try to apply to a situation a form conceived in advance, although patterns of growth have much in common and one can build up a knowledge of man and child which serves as a flexible method. This kind of seasoning occurs in every craft. The teacher tries to work in relation to the child's temperament, not against it. He tries to help the child toward his individuality. This is what no teacher must sin against. He helps the child to be free of the ignorance and fear and clumsiness and compulsive treachery which may oppress his being. It is a terrible thing when a teacher gives the impression that he does not care what a child does. It is false and it is unfaithful. The child hopes that an adult will have more sense and more heart than that. The teacher therefore seeks to understand what the child hungers for in the life of his imagination, his mind, his senses, his emotions, his will. This means that he does not take things at their face value but sees elements in relation to a lifetime process of deep structures.

The teacher helps the child to live into art and knowledge as into a single realm. When the powers of the child-artist are transformed into the powers of the argumentative youth, imagination and concreteness imbue the powers of abstract thinking which tend normally to bloom in puberty. Likewise, the teacher does not separate reverence from will. The child's tenderness is continuously encouraged and extended throughout his observations and behavior. We do not want to be gifted boors when we grow up. We do not want to be mannerly nincompoops. We want the quick of our life to stand in our surfaces. Moral precepts are of little use to a child. Human example is more convincing.

The experience of metamorphosis runs through nature, and through man as part of nature. We see in different stages of a person's life how certain abilities are ascendant, others dormant. A time for tilling, a time for harvesting, a time for lying fallow. The preschool child is busy with physical growth: he crawls, he stands upright, he speaks, he begins the change of teeth; the child-body is in almost constant motion: asserting, imitating. The child takes in his world as if it were food. And his world nourishes or starves him. Nothing escapes his thirst. Secrets are impossible. He identifies with his surroundings, and they live within him unconsciously; it is perhaps for this reason that the small child has been characterized as naturally religious.

Since the very soul of the child's surroundings comes to life in his body, the early years are drastic in their relation to later health. They help to shape the body's hardness or softness, tension or ease. In later years these tendencies are transformed into the sickness or health of the adult, in whom it is likewise impossible to distinguish between body and soul: between the living being and the shape it takes. The child of an angry parent may in later life develop digestive disorders. The child of an indifferent parent may develop respiratory disorders. A phlegmatic teacher may do another kind of damage. Of course the sins of the fathers are visited upon the children, and we are all both children and fathers. The task is very difficult: to foster in children those qualities which will mature into blessings rather than afflictions. It is not within our power to do everything we dream of doing. We must be patient and diligent and hold faithfully before our vision the ideals we serve, no matter how long it may take to accomplish them.

This feeling for the ideal is natural to children. They are alert to fraud, intimidation, insincerity, perhaps because they indulge in them so freely. They know by instinct that there is a real thing and a fake. This was expressed unforgettably for me by a young girl with whom I was driving across country. As we passed through a small town, she saw a cemetery on the main street. "Is that a real cemetery or just for show?" she asked.

Children have as well a natural feeling for their own worth and for meaningfulness. (And may we be forgiven any injury we do to these, by making them the butt of jokes they do not understand or by foisting off our cynicism upon their tender beginnings.) When I visited my nephew, age four, I mentioned how much he had grown since I had seen him last. "Oh," he replied, "I'm bigger than this!" And he was right. I'm bigger than this! And may I be helped to grow to my full size. How can we know ourselves as men without knowing ourselves as children? For that spirit is in us.

Another imperishable remark from a child's lips which serves me was made by a little boy with whom I was discussing the various routes we could take to the zoo. I was spinning it out. "You can go however you like," he agreed, "but you have to get there." True, true. We can go however we like, but we have to get there.

The human organism is delicate as well as tough. Its moods are lyric as well as dramatic as well as epic. It contains within itself the history of its race; and in the education of its consciousness, this history is resummoned. The child grows through, as it were, his own history as a human being into his future as a unique individual.

A child should not be encouraged to think abstractly nor to judge nor to become intellectually precocious nor to read books before his powers of observation are well developed. Certain tendencies we should try to cure, others to strengthen. We should not neglect the child's relation to hero worship and ceremony and ritual. He lives naturally in a world of myth and poetry and invisible beings. He loves sound and movement and color and drama. He loves to laugh and to cry. Whatever we teach him should be touched by the spirit of the world that is natural to him. As he grows older and learns to think abstractly, he will do so as a person in whose organism is rooted the wisdom of fairy tales, and saints' legends, and cultural mythology, and the experience of number in music and dance and handwork, and the experience of fantasy in poetry and painting and drama, and the acuteness of observation of the natural world of plants and animals and people nowhere so stunning as in the child.

Participation in history and society grows out of myth, legend, biography, nature study. The sense of language grows out of motion and gesture and picture and sound. A sense of the earth and its resources grows out of a kinship with its living surfaces and depths. And the teacher should aid in this education *personally* — not by textbook! (The children should make their own.) The knowledge he may convey then will be infused with human qualities of imagination and sensory delight and true concern. The acts of manhood will have been nourished by living sources. This is the hope. The alternatives appear to be estrangement, sterility, moral lunacy. However bohemian or bourgeois the cut.

A teacher is at a disadvantage who is not deeply sensitive to the nature of his pupil. Some may, for example, be concerned for a child's freedom, yet be unable to share his anxieties, or enjoy his noise, his candor, his affection and innocence. They may admire the poetry written by adults for children, but be quite ignorant of how the poetic impulse manifests in children themselves. This is perhaps why it is said that a good teacher is taught by his students. For he is not to teach them merely what he knows but to help to bring to maturity what is already in them. It takes, of course, a very good ear, to hear what is present in a child, or an adult.

We teachers have to strive to perfect ourselves in generosity and imagination and the ability to identify ourselves with others. Teaching should contain in it neither disdain nor disinterest. It is for this reason that a teacher must yield himself over and over again to the imagination of his pupil so that it may be brought to fruitfulness.

Let us acknowledge that a school is more than a place or a staff or a student body; it is a process: of bringing to birth, of awakening. Teacher-training within the school is most valuable, and our immaturity as teachers may require that at certain times we be primarily concerned with our own education. At best the process is reciprocal. There deserves to be a careful and continuous preparation. It is important to remember, when we are making a school, that education is a very ancient art indeed, and that the community of scholars is vast. Participation within it should be one of our conscious aims.

To be deeply understood, Pedagogy needs to be seen not as an activity nor a livelihood, but as a centering discipline in which teacher and learner are mutually committed.

My own style of teaching is probably reflected in the principles and moods of this book. It is based upon the physical foundation of the clay body, infused with invisible spirit. I am committed to substance, to innerness, to moral evolution. Whether I am teaching pottery or English, to children or adults, I am trying for free perception, free initiative, free participation.

Free perception leads the senses freely to follow the movement of form as it occurs, unobstructed by habit, anxiety, or unconcern.

Free initiative is based upon self-knowledge, and is a fruit of maturity. A child should not be asked to cast himself free of what he has not yet become. By initiative I mean an ability to create a future uncoerced by the past. An adult may develop an awareness of purpose (emerging form) underlying the thin stratum of his conscious designs, go beyond his taste, surmount the consequences of training and experience, and cast himself futureward toward the unknown. All these elements in himself he recenters in a larger sphere.

Free participation is the ability to unite with others, to collaborate, to identify. It may be developed through the community aspect of a school or a workshop or any group into which life has cast one. It means an ability to work with whatever human materials are at hand and is therefore basically artistic in nature. It means a sense of spontaneity, of seeing the originality of each instant and each person, of permitting the relationships that exist in a situation to press their claim.

To live as artists in the moods and materials of life! To use our plasticity, yet to seek the truth of being and inner form that belong to us individually as a living clay vessel, to discover and to take our form in freedom and obedience. Not to sell ourselves short as less interesting, less beautiful and stirring and mysterious than the things we make — less visionary and hopeful and intact. And to realize that we do not win our depth and our inner form and our texture and our truth of being without the fire. Ordeal by fire. There is no substitute for transformation of the body.

Education is personal. At the outset I lay my cards on the table. I speak about my life, my history, my interests, my activities, my tastes and limitations, my point of view, my intentions. I ask for a similar candor. The world is bigger than one's teacher. And no one knows it better than I. But sometimes there is in a classroom a kind of mock-piety, which pretends that everything important is being done there. Ridiculous! I try to destroy the falsely routine and to create a fresh and mutual respect. I work at both poles, reassuring and inciting. I want the students to be spontaneous and energetic; at the same time I want them to be sensitive and aware and composed. I want them to be on fire; at the same time I want the flames to be healing. I want the flame of life, out of which the phoenix is born. Fire in the stone, which purifies, transforms, enkindles.

So I tug and nip, bark and jump, and never take my eyes away. Even when I am most still, most elsewhere occupied, most free of interest in them, I am present. I care, and eventually they come to know it. Sometimes it is a long fight before they yield to me their hope. I believe in this way: by the quality of our attention and our wit, to foster contact and independence.

I tell them reading requires love and detachment. Writing, warmth and perspective. To understand what something is, we have to observe it very carefully: listen, look, touch, smell, taste, imagine, feel. We must leave nothing out. Henry James said that a writer is a person upon whom nothing is lost. Well, anybody should be: a person upon whom nothing is lost!

Appreciation requires a discipline of selflessness. I tell them the expression of personal taste is not our primary goal. The development of taste is: the ability to taste what is present. I try to exercise this sleeping or lethargic member by making it clear that I am not primarily concerned with what we like. I am concerned with our power to grasp, to comprehend, to penetrate, and to embrace. There are different levels at work here as elsewhere. It is not possible to learn anything without enjoyment. On the other hand, there is an attachment to liking and disliking that obstructs learning and deeper enjoyment. The right to opinion must be honored without exception, but not all opinions are equally honorable. Though everyone is free to be who he is, ignorance and cruelty are not freedoms.

Fine discrimination requires a discipline of non-discrimination, of affirmation. Awareness of the world must precede its registration. For this reason I find so timely now the invasion of the West by Oriental philosophy, which stresses non-attachment and other modes of being by which systems of evaluation may be transcended. Western man needs help in using his organism's unconscious flow. He seems to have developed a differentiated consciousness at the expense of a fertilizing contact with the "ground" of being. He needs to let go of the intellectualism which tends to be the spirit of our art and theology as well as our research.

So at the same time that I encourage personal response, I urge that personal response be enlarged to where it is willing to take in more and more of the universe. Of course this meets resistance. Why not? But it is a teacher's skill to disarm resistance, just as it is a student's to understand his own. We learn to take risks, to lay it on the line. We express our feelings. For we cannot read nor hear if we are bored and hostile and confused. We contract, energy freezes.

However, once the energy is flowing, there is still more to be done. Our organisms must be able to dance, but they must also be able to be quiet with the same sense of energy and release, unreduced. In this stillness we listen. The more alive and quieter we are, the better we hear, the better we read. This is meditation. As we listen to each other, as we enter into dialogue, we find our personal reactions transformed into a sense of a larger reality which far transcends our previous likes and dislikes. Perception has altered the quality of our consciousness. As consciousness expands to the size of reality, character seems to strengthen. We are more able to act in the light of our awareness. Thus may character be affected through education.

As consciousness heightens, the moral sense evolves. We learn to be human beings through studying nature and man. There has to be in our pedagogy this dialogue between release of energy and direction of energy — between following pleasure and following wisdom; for the fullest release comes when the right direction is found, and the tenderest rapture comes in the depths of law. Otherwise, when we are grown up and can do as we please, though we may see what needs to be done, we will have no firm will to do it. Our bodies will be unready to assume the forms of our visions. And we will live in fantasy.

Everyone talks about love. And I talk about it as much as anyone. I think love is fostered by a capacity to experience cosmos. We educate ourselves and others to enjoy the "suchness" of things: the special flavor of each particular instant of being: induplicable, numinous. When we have this capacity strong within us, then will be time enough to talk about love.

To say Yes Yes to what we behold! To what is witless, depraved, ugly, vacant, and to what is graceful, endearing, and noble — equally. It will not do to leave out the violence we cannot bear — the intimacy, the banality, the blasphemy, the holiness we cannot bear. It simply will not do.

It is difficult to understand and to love creation. We seek therefore to be modest and patient with ourselves as with others. We do not shake our fist at an infant learning to walk, and shout, "What, not walking yet? Must be some kind of a dumbbell!" We know how long it takes to be born, and to stand upright, and to walk; and no matter how steady on our legs we may become, we may yet slip and fall. We may hurt ourselves, and if we are lucky, someone will help us to our feet and comfort our pain and embarrassment. Hope is physical in people's faces, and works its stress through the resistant membranes to expression.

The capacity for fellowship is larger than personal liking. It is an openness to life which does not negate. To be open to what we see and hear, in our reading and writing, our receiving and giving: this is one aim of our pedagogy.

Our public acts will be those of private men in a common undertaking. Our courtesy will not falter, but extend from center to periphery, including all within.

As we grow to life size, our perceptions widen and deepen and grow finer in detail. A curious thing happens: and again I grasp it through a potter's image. As we come to contain reality as our inner shape, we "fall into round." We take the shape in which we are originally "thrown." Awareness and behavior fuse; inner and outer dissolve to transparency.

Centering is reflected in a community impulse within a class. I try in the first meetings to develop a sense of fellowship and mutual service. An assortment of strangers may learn to speak directly to one another, turning gradually into a sensitively attuned body of men, who have warmth of feeling and courageous discernment. They find how to learn and to teach. In them grows a relish for the special qualities of individuals, so that any class may feel how it benefits by the presence of all. Individuals may learn to rejoice in what they do not themselves possess but which they can recognize as capacities of life.

A standardized concept of intelligence is misleading. Even those individuals who are ordinarily deemed handicapped have a sensitivity which engenders unique responses (hence values) in other living beings. Their intuitive and yielding natures are instructive to those of us who are brash with good health. The interrelation of temperaments in a group of people is in itself highly educative. A class with different levels of aptitude and many kinds of response may bloom like a garden, full of color and texture. Every one has something to give the others. Every one may learn to receive from others. An atmosphere of helpfulness and realism may flourish. Also the timid ones may gain in confidence as they come to understand what their contribution is, and the bold, assured ones may gain in tenderness and sensitivity. It seems to me that a class should live as an example of the precepts we teach about equality and fraternity. For the teacher, everything and everyone is grist to the mill. For the person likewise. Techniques develop out of the living practices of centering.

Different modes of knowing exist within us. But rarely does formal education seek a balance between them. We are asked to explain, to justify, to cite causes; we are asked to defend our point of view, and to prove. And proof, we are assured, is always sense-perceptible or logically demonstrable. We tend to hold our intuitive gifts in low esteem.

Perhaps it is because in handcraft one works more immediately with material and less with concepts about it, in organic rhythms suitable to the natural materials one is handling, that one gets to know one's material in something like an intuitive way. One may develop a capacity for experiencing other phenomena in this way: in immediacy, listening to something that is not audible but that nevertheless one hears, responding to the nature of being. Responding to the nature of A Being. Not to his words alone, nor to his look alone, not to any partial aspect: responding to the total organism-presence, as if he were a work of art. Imbued with life, we live into a relationship, we live into an understanding. The craftsman works from an immediate life sense. There is little reason in our culture to make pottery or furniture or fabric or jewelry by hand except out of an intuitive sense of one's own being and the being of others, and a love for the work. Surely there is no social or economic reason: no status, not much money, no security. The self-employed craftsman may labor upon his own nature and upon his fibers and ores with a special kind of realism. Society needs the spirit of the craftsman throughout its procedures. For material prosperity and professional success, which are so much touted, often fall short of satisfying the person as much as he had been led to expect. There have been so many inner compromises, so many moments of falseness in the interests of expediency and the public image, that by the time the body is well dressed and housed and fed and delighted, the simple heart will have gone out of it. Working in the crafts can help to make a man bold in his honor, perhaps because he has very little else to lose!

It is a mistake to offer awareness as the goal of education, in the sense it is usually meant. It settles, not for deep knowledge of being, but a superficial recognition that certain things exist. Dissatisfaction among college students is notorious. They hear that college is the road to fulfillment. And the most they get is a ticket into a job, and enough knowledge of the problems of life to be worried and indecisive, but not enough to be active on behalf of their ideals. Man does not live by bread alone? Well, and what else does he need? The implication is that man needs not only security but freedom, not only survival but rebirth.

Unfortunately, even the dream of freedom as popularly peddled misses the point. Freedom, the patter goes, is the right to do as one pleases as long as it doesn't bother anybody else. But everything one does "bothers" in some sense somebody or indeed everybody else. We are a real and radiating presence in the environment, no matter how quietly we may stand. The atmosphere we poison blows among all men equally.

Man is a physical creature, energetic in nature: his thoughts, his feelings, his motives, his secret innermost heart and private dreams are physical entities charged with energy, and man gives off this energy in the form it has taken just as surely as he gives off the old air from his lungs or the moisture from his skin. There is no moment without importance. And human beings are equipped to receive sensations whether or not conscious and measurable communication is taking place. Teachers should remember this. For the teacher gives off himself; in a sense what he is projecting into the class is himself. A knowledgeable but cynical teacher can rob a subject of its bloom and damage the soul of his class. A warm and trusting teacher can rouse into life whatever he touches — he can inspire.

The distance which may exist between a teacher's professed values and the example of his life is often smoothed over by enthusiastic reference to how aware he is, how bright. It took me a long time to realize that the awareness I am interested in, for myself as for others, reaches into the will. It took me a long time, but perhaps no longer than it normally takes to mature through the stages of apprenticeship. One emerges from one's past as from a crysalis — at a threshhold of futurity. Everything is subtly changed. One looks with a fond distance at the corpse in which one grew. Perhaps one may now learn to serve the world in one's new form.

The old saw that life begins at forty has its basis in fact. For in maturity occurs a natural birth of a selfhood which has been growing within the womb of spirit. The generative principle never ceases. It is for this reason that I find metamorphosis a more useful image for understanding history than I do an image of rising and falling cultures. Seasons rise and fall. The man grows by their means.

110

It was a long time before I felt reborn within myself the intuitions natural to child-hood, when freedom is a loyalty to life. Grown-ups do not always mean what they say. It takes awhile to recover those faculties we had as children to see into the heart.

I began consciously to turn toward the wisdom of pottery at a time of breakdown of other values. It was a major life-shock for me to discover that the community I had chosen, that of artists and teachers and worshipers, was as flawed as the rest of society. "Mortal men, mortal men / fit to fill a pit with" — as Jack Falstaff once said of the soldiers in his company. The world is full of great books, and we had read some of them. As educated persons we taught the language of nobility — and remained ourselves small. How could it be? I and my fellows had taken the highest degrees at the academy and in good faith had sought a path to the good life, and yet found ourselves in the middle of our age "in a darkling wood astray," in moral vacuity, emotional rout, intellectual non-commitment, imaginative ennui. Literate, and imbecile. How could it be? By what science were we to understand ourselves?

Of course it was my mistake: a misconception fed by sentimentality, ignorance, vanity. I learned my lesson. And I learned it by living through a breakdown of most of the systems I had received from my education. I faced in disbelief and rage and despair the reality that Higher Education had not equipped me nor my colleagues with human insight nor a loving will. Knowledge had not ennobled our behavior. I wrestled with this riddle through a long night of years. I have come to the experience and image of centering after serving my time in Hell.

When I speak angrily about human weakness or urgently about human possibility, I do not contradict my faith in life's destructive element. Again it is a matter of levels. There is a level of being in which creation and destruction separate and interact, serving mu-tually the increase of perception. My desire for health does not blind me to the meaning-fulness of sickness. For again there is a level of being in which sickness and health act dynamically to foster the growth of capacities. Life is very complex indeed. And the polari-ties always function in relation to each other. We know how anguish may precede a blessed transformation. We live by a marvelous physics: there is a spirit of form shaping us as surely as it shapes the crystal or the bee.

Our mistakes carry a wisdom in them. Our resistances as well. As, in the apprecia-tion of literature, personal taste must be carefully handled, so at the level of our highest human concern, our personal reaction is not so interesting as our ability to be free of it. One does not expect to like instinctively all the persons one meets. One does expect to work diligently to be free to enjoy whoever comes one's way. I believe passionately in this discipline: to achieve a position at center which enables one to experience the multiple forms of existence.

Part of the excitement is that there are forms one cannot risk without collapse. Nor can we be fulfilled without the fire. We must be brave and skillful and prudent. A certain amount of mistreatment may give us an interesting surface, but too much rough handling will ruin us. We are perishable. My sense of spiritual continuum in no way weakens my sense of the peril we are in. My joy embraces my terror. I live but by paradox. And therefore I am freest when I am most centered in the void.

This story is told about the Buddha, who one day was sought out by an ardent follower who had brought presents to the master to show his devotion. The Buddha gave him audience. The man stepped forward and held out his right hand, offering a priceless ivory ornament. "Drop it," said Buddha. The man, surprised, stepped back. Then he stepped forward again, this time offering in his left hand a precious jewel. "Drop it," said Buddha. Again the disciple, surprised, obeyed and stepped back. Then, smiling as if catching the Buddha's meaning, he held out both hands empty and stepped forward. "Drop it," said Buddha.

What do we prize most: our doubt? our talent? our privacy? our independence? our personality? friendship? integrity? purposelessness? . . . ? It must all be laid aside, consciously and voluntarily. One's hands must be empty if they are to receive. Empty if they are to give. Empty even of emptiness.

In spirit, the artist (by whom I mean man in his creating aspect) like the saint (by whom I mean man in his adoring aspect) gives away all he has: possessions and human ties — in order to be open before Presence. Or, if you prefer, in order to be constructive. This act is, in its own way, destructive of worldly forms. I see forms constantly perishing in the perpetuation of life. This is the spirit of regeneration. It works within us constantly. Let us cooperate with it, finding in it the fulfillment of our love. It is a sacrifice. It is a sacrament, celebrating the mystery of matter.

We have to teach these things, to ourselves first of all, and to others. To throw oneself with gusto into the swim of events and processes. To learn to love all things so that one can love each thing. To realize that the separations of life are the dynamics of union. To the mind this may seem like a paradox, but it is no paradox to the organism's consciousness of growth. We do not have to start at the beginning every time. History has given many examples to help us. Art and literature and revelation also. Philosophy and science and law. We do not work without aid.

The lonely soul labors toward fraternity. He labors to free himself from pride and ignorance and sloth so that he may live as a brother to other men. It is a lifelong task. Community life helps in this process. Mutual effort and understanding, practiced over a long period in the earnest spirit of a discipline, tend to help us toward our freedom. Certain jobs can be done only together, for a society of men provides a sinew no man has alone. People need each other in order that out of the multitude a whole image may be formed. The dialogue of our strengths and weaknesses, if we keep it alive and flowing, may allow compassion to grow naturally. Community is a basic instructive force and is therefore fundamental to pedagogy.

The dialogue runs not only among individuals, but among groups and nations. Can we in our schools change the race from "get" to "give"? We say we want peace, but are we willing to give up our way of life in order to make peace possible? Or do we want it spread like gravy over the turkey? Are we willing to give what we have to those who need? Are we willing to take no more thought for what we shall eat and what we shall wear than do the lilies of the field? Will we bestow our goods upon even "the least" of men: "the undeserving poor," as Dorothy Day of the Catholic Worker Movement ruefully calls the derelicts she spends her energy and prayers upon?

The needs of the Person have to be met. They are not being met; our madhouses and hospitals are overcrowded. People are squeezed and split between inner and outer pressures, until at the conscious level they can hardly feel anything any more. Doctors try to relieve the pressures by confessional purges, chemical sedatives, and libidinal release. Tranquilizer, stimulant, escape hatch — still the hunger and hysteria and indifference grow.

Let us teach in our classes the connection between who we think man is on the inside and what the atmosphere is like on the outside. For "ideas have consequences." If we put self-disregard or self-interest above a reverence for life, we will kill ourselves just as surely as if we were blowing ourselves up with a bomb. What's the difference? Humanity can kill itself without lifting a finger, without even pressing a button. All it has to do is turn itself off. And then get "kicks" by "turning on." The picture is everywhere to be seen. Genocide. The bomb is only a detail. The big boom on the firecracker we've been fiddling with for centuries. The mess in social justice, the mess in medicine, the mess in agriculture, the mess in foods and drugs, the mess in education are symptoms of the mess in the human soul. Who do we think we are? Meat with hairs growing out of it, as a friend of mine suggested? What is man? What is a man's work, what is a man's pleasure? What do we want to be when we grow up? Is sexual satisfaction our goal in life? or financial security? or emotional security? or freedom from concern for others? I mean, what are we educating ourselves *for*? We are on our way somewhere, but where? Do we care? Henry David Thoreau says it is our duty as citizens to disobey unjust laws. Fill the jails to overflowing, he says. Do we dare? We teach Thoreau's writings in our schools. Why do we not fill our jails in protest against unwise laws? Where are the independence and freedom and individualism we are forever prating about in our schools? It seems to me that on the contrary we are ruled by fear of authority and social pressure, masquerading as majority rule.

It was a little child who said, "But the emperor has no clothes on," when all the populace were falsely and hypnotically praising his fine robes. Be ye as a little child.

Everyone was aware that the emperor had no clothes on, but they were keeping silent. They weren't saying anything that could be used against them. Why? Out of deference to the emperor's insanity? What kind of witchcraft is it that educates our awareness and paralyzes our wills? It is this question of the will, of the lived value, which must enter vitally into education today.

Now it is not always possible to gather free will impulses from one's environment, and one's own nature is not always bearing the fruit one would wish. A man grows up and finds himself caught in a tangle of forces and values which are obstructive to life. How to get out? How is he to behave freely? It is not enough to teach slogans, we must teach techniques.

I would look for an answer to this question in a study of the imagination. And I would place the development of imagination among the primary goals of education.

Imagination is the ability to picture in the mind what is not present to the senses. It is the faculty by which we perceive what we have not observed nor experienced. It is that power which characterizes the poet as Wordsworth describes him: "to be affected by absent things as if they were present; . . . expressing . . . especially those thoughts and feelings which, by his own choice, or from the structure of his own mind, arise in him without immediate external excitement." It is the ability to behold living images which are not sense-perceptible. Values, when imagined, are not derived from present elements, but are beheld in the spiritual realm, as if an organ were functioning to produce not physical cells but spiritual tissue.

The seed of this power exists in the child's capacity to picture for himself a story one is telling him. By the rapt expression on his face, one can almost see what he is seeing. A pedagogical technique emphasized by Rudolph Steiner is that teachers present knowledge to the child first through his imagination, and later follow it with empirical observation. First the earth's plants are described, then the nature walk is taken. First the monuments of culture are presented in imaginative pictures, then the trip to the museum is taken. Thus information is a documentation of what one knows. Life is experienced inwardly, in consciousness. Things are its manufacture; they embody and reflect.

From the child's capacity to imagine grows as well the adult's capacity for compassion: the ability to picture the sufferings of others, to identify. In one's citizenship, or the art of politics, it is part of one's skill to imagine other ways of living than one's own. Certain experiences are knowable only through imagination. It is a mode of perception, and may lead to acts of initiative as well as to artistic vision.

Imagination in the craftsman works in various ways. There is much to ponder on here. He does not always build toward a prior vision. Often images come in the process of working. The material, his hands — together they beget. The craftsman experiences Form as a continuous force. He experiences how forms come, unsummoned. How matter itself, when it is imbued with life in his hand, continuously takes form. Once we know in our flesh that the world is imbued throughout with formative energy, we begin to experience how alive the world is, the air is, the earth is, we are. How full of possibilities. Once we begin to grasp how illusory are our certainties and uncertainties, we can begin to enjoy our doubts as symptoms in the process of knowledge. It is this Negative Capability which John

Keats was so struck by as that quality which goes to form "a Man of Achievement, especially in Literature, and which Shakespeare possessed so enormously . . . that is, when a man is capable of being in uncertainties, mysteries, doubts, without any irritable reaching after fact and reason."

In other moments, the craftsman works from an inner vision which has dwelt in his imagination and has perhaps impelled him to his studio. I think it is useful to distinguish between these moods of ready vision and of groping. In our teaching we need to appeal to whichever capacity requires strengthening as well as to urge on that which leads. The person who is anxious or careless when he doesn't know what he is doing, or the person who is bored and restless unless he is improvising or working by chance — both will benefit by relaxing their vigilance. For they are equally involved in paradox. No matter how we rehearse our intention, the performance has its own accidents. And though we may prefer indeterminacy, we are determined in our preference and find that we are surprising almost nobody with our surprises. Because of the law of polarity, if we devote ourselves too exclusively to one pole, our world will tend to go flat. It is not a formula we are involved in, but a mystery. As I began by saying in this book, as soon as we find ourselves attached too consistently to one procedure, one response, we owe it to ourselves to move consciously into another field. Otherwise we may dull our ear for the whole.

In his poem "The Excursion" William Wordsworth has written a passage which suggests the magnitude of our listening power:

> I have seen
> A curious child, who dwelt upon a tract
> Of inland ground, applying to his ear
> The convolutions of a smooth-lipped shell;
> To which, in silence hushed, his very soul
> Listened intensely; and his countenance soon
> Brightened with joy; for from within were heard
> Murmurings, whereby the monitor expressed
> Mysterious union with its native sea.
> Even such a shell the universe itself
> Is to the ear of Faith; and there are times,
> I doubt not, when to you it doth impart

Authentic tidings of invisible things;
Of ebb and flow, and ever-during power;
And central peace, subsisting at the heart
Of endless agitation.

The ear of Faith is, I suggest, the ear of one who keeps faith with the agitation and the peace, and who, through the sacrament of his body, experiences their union. The ear of Faith is, to my hearing, neither deaf nor slavish. It does not falsify, nor does it reduce the tidings to explanation. If it aspires to convey what it hears, it re-composes, for the EAR. The body of man is a listening chamber; it is a lyre, which reverberates. Any instrument is, in a sense, an ear, in that it responds to impact, whether of breath or stroke. You can think of the world as a vast orchestra astir with sound, its strings and chambers and disks set into motion by motion. But the strings and chambers are already moving, already alive. An orchestra of living instruments whose capacities to hear and to resound are transformed through processes of growth.

We play what we hear. Is this not a useful image of man? He plays what he hears. And what he hears plays through him from the impact of the world upon him and from the nature of his instrument. Thus he has the double adventure of knowing himself and of studying the forces that play upon him.

An ability to receive is an ability to hear. If we are good receivers, through us may play the music of the spheres. The relation of receiving to responding is yet another dimension of Moral Acoustics. There is, I think, a sense in which our deeds are shaped by the ear of Faith, as Wordsworth called it. There is a deep sense in which those "authentic tidings of invisible things" bear to us the physical impulses of our moral form. If we keep faith with what we truly hear, at our center, in our ear's EAR, we may better serve an ideal of quest and compassion.

The polarities of creation and destruction have been basic to my discussion so far. Dialogue between these two voices is the motif of education. The surrealists put it drastically: "THE NEGATIVE TASKS OF POETRY ARE NOT LESS IMPORTANT THAN ITS POSITIVE TASKS, THEY ARE INDISSOLUBLY LINKED ONE TO THE OTHER. THE SINE QUA NON OF THE REINTEGRATION OF MAN IS THE DISINTEGRATION OF THE PRESENT HUMAN CONDITION."

The utmost disordering prepares the way for the birth of new forms, new awareness of new depths and interpenetrations. Destruction is desirable, not in the spirit of nihilism but in the knowledge of the regenerative process.

"Let them burn the library at Alexandria," cried Artaud. "It is good that our excessive facilities be no longer available, that forms fall into oblivion: a culture without space or time, limited only by the capacity of our own nerves, will reappear with all the more energy. It is right that from time to time cataclysms occur which compel us to return to nature, i.e. to rediscover life."

Of course this is no more drastic than the practice of modern science to create power through the disintegration of matter. If you remember your genetics, you will recall that before the birth of a new cell, a disorganization (or what appears to our eyes as such) of cell structure occurs. The chromosomes go crazy, everything is unrecognizable; then, all of a sudden, something new; the body is intact and changed. You have to study nature if you want to know what is going on. There is a law at work, of that there seems little doubt.

Experiments are being conducted in the arts and pedagogy as well as physics, to test its operation. Every banner declares the same: Freedom.

When we say that education works toward freeing the person, we are saying more than we can implement. Here as elsewhere, we serve an ideal. The ideal works through the polarities of release and discipline. Energies continuously play, spending and husbanding themselves, expanding and contracting like a huge bellows playing upon a fire. We do not want libidinal exhaustion, nor do we want superego constipation. We don't want social confusion and cultural frivolity, nor do we want pedantic tidiness and pious propriety. We have to keep the energies alive and playing; this is part of our pedagogy.

The dominant image of our time is the freeing of energy by nuclear explosion. It is a living out of the law of distintegration and creation, as if this era of destruction were to precede a penetration into the inner reality of our cosmos of which modern man has scarcely dreamed. To get past the outer form of the nucleus — since he has not the clairvoyance to see through it — he has had to bombard it to bits. What he finds on the inside of matter may bring him into a science which will free the inner life of man immeasurably by enlarging the field of consciousness.

Be that as it may, I know something about how this law of destruction and creation works from having spent several years at a self-determining college, as a member of its faculty, participating in an experiment in curriculum and community. The example of

Black Mountain College, somewhat in the news from 1933 to 1957, bears upon our concern here. It based itself upon Person rather than upon trade, and it tried to integrate individual spirit and community spirit. It also tried to give teachers freedom to do what they wished and at the same time to satisfy students. It put art at the center of the curriculum, no matter what the major field of study might be.

The first announcement of the college stated, "We have found that often through working in one of the arts, students are led to an intellectual awakening more effectively than in any other way." The processes of art, as Steiner had pointed out years earlier, are a paradigm for other processes mistakenly deemed intellectual. The resourcefulness and enjoyment characteristic in the arts were discovered to be equally relevant to intellectual and social aims.

It was basically a centering problem. How to bring elements into a whole which could move in a variety of ways without falling apart. This process can occur only with plastic substance; it cannot occur if elements are unyielding.

There is a tendency nowadays to think that "process" is the heart of the matter. Magic is looked for in activity itself. What I have learned is that materials are a condition of process. We cannot make a new situation unless we are prepared to let go of what we hold most dear. And newness is not given by the succession of instants. Substance may be changed, for example dissolved, by time; and yet its mineral character remain unchanged. In order for substance really to change, there must be transformation in its character. This is a matter of innerness, of *content*.

When John Andrew Rice founded Black Mountain College, after an academic-freedom ruckus at Rollins College where he had been professor of classics, he based it on principles which would make a conventional institution impossible. No property, no rank, no tenure, no board of trustees, no president, no grades, no endowment. Just the faculty and students, a cook, a handyman, and a building rented from September to June. Later the college bought property and developed a year-round program, but this was after Rice had left. The effect of this environment was to pulverize the forms of behavior to which one had been previously educated. If you were supple enough to yield to the invasion of a new reality, you had a good chance to be reinvested. If you tightened and withdrew, you might escape, but you might also get a bad fall. If you just stood there, you might go into shock or you might go fishing.

The separations and disharmonies of our culture flowed into the college community, and it wrestled to transform them into a living organism which was whole and unseparated. Ordinary dualisms dissolved: faculty and student, school and society, thought and life, intellect and character, knowledge and inspiration, fine and useful arts, professional and amateur, pass and fail, underclassman and graduate, laborer and egghead, work and play, riches and poverty. These were no longer useful categories. A conventional system of distinctions tended to be threatened. This threat made life raw and tough and earnest.

Teachers had no status other than as persons. They lived in spirit as one family with the students. Privacy was illusory. One came to one's class naked to the scrutiny of all.

Decisions were ours to make, publicity ours to write, money ours to raise. There was no one to blame. We could do what we wanted. We could create an educational community which would be open, flexible, contemporary, humane. Or so we supposed, since there was no external control. The average teaching load was six hours a week. Life was custom-built.

The disintegrating effect of this kind of freedom is classic. You find that most of your thinking has been reactive, and that your powers for original decision are undeveloped. It is very difficult in this situation not to import the patterns of old rivalries, not to find them lingering like deposits in the soul. It is very difficult to abandon all one's former supports and to move forward into unfamiliar contacts. There are almost no handles in the situation except one's own bootstraps. When you can do what you want to do, what will you do?

This also I learned: destruction may be complete. One may perish. Or one may depart and simply perpetuate oneself. No transformation will have taken place.

At Black Mountain College, the centering impulse was strong, consciously or unconsciously. One way dualisms were transcended was by making it clear that members of the college were themselves bipolar. Teachers attended each other's classes and were thereby students. Faculty served on dish crews, coal crews, road crews, farm crews, and were thereby laborers. Students tried their hands at teaching, in areas where they had experience and where there was a need. What a person could do, he did. Contribution was not standardized. One looked for the spot where one could be most effective or where one had most to learn. Almost anything was possible, if it were seriously undertaken.

Thus the person had movable functions as did the college. Each was a many-membered being. If you start with organism, then multiple functions do not destroy the unity. Also, if you start with organism, then locus or place is not so important. For you lose no centeredness by having a movable site. This was one of the most remarkable proposals made during the last days of the struggle to meet the financial obligations contingent upon place: that the college become *mobile*. It would operate "three periods of four months annually in travelling operations, following the seasons. Two of these periods to be spent in two separate single locations (variable from year to year) and the third period to be spent on the road travelling from place to place. . . . That the college live in tents and by similar transient means, and it travel its whole operation, including equipment, library, etc., by means of trailers, cars, etc." A college that would be not a place but a making, *poein*, by persons, engaged with each other and with data!

This form would be naturally "thrown" out of a body where curriculum is art. Concrete experiences in thinking-with-the-organism, integrating perception and imagination and physical coordination — requiring study, observation, initiative, an ability to invent and to put things together. The curriculum as a whole is created, like art, to deepen the image of man, to make discoveries. And one thing every artist knows is how much hard physical labor is involved in making something new. A community where art is a central discipline is likely to develop an exceptional realism about the work to be done.

Since students and teachers as well came from all over the United States and the world, the interpenetrations in this small community (largest: 125 persons; smallest: 15) had the dimensions and force of what is often referred to as "the outside world." After attending such a school, no young adult is surprised to learn that food has to be provided, dishes done, sheets laundered, cows milked, milk skimmed and cooled, floors mopped, roads maintained, roofs repaired, children loved, guests housed ,crises met, books mended, windows caulked, solitude respected, differences enjoyed, cooperation required, spontaneity used, judgments made and revised, help given by all to all, patience won. It comes as no surprise that warfare can go on only if there is an underlying commitment to peace. Quarreling and dissension constitute a release of energy and vindication of ego, but to be useful they must be companioned by tolerance and forgiveness.

It is an incomparable satisfaction to share in an environment where one may perform all one's functions in a milieu of relationship. The arts of the person and of society fuse, as do private and public decorum. If each person has an equal voice in government and an equal right to life, liberty, and the pursuit of happiness, then majority rule alone won't do. For this reason, at Black Mountain College, voting was unpopular. The group sought a "sense of the meeting." Ideally, action was taken only when unanimous agreement had been reached..

The centeredness or unity of such a life is a consequence of the curriculum, in which art and communitas share the hegemony with intellectual skills. Where making is a central activity, every example has value: making bread, making a sign, making a report, making a table, making a concert, making love, making tea, making a baseball game, making plans for next year, *making*. In making, we develop a feel for materials, for the play between purpose and accident and inspiration, for gestalt, for instrument, for becoming, for death as physical process essential to creation; and we are filled with wonder.

Since the chief material in education is human — the student who seeks, the teacher who likewise seeks but has an experience which makes him a useful guide — we must apply ourselves to a study of man and his needs. It is no use to say that we would none of us go to school if we didn't have to, for education takes place as experience takes place.

Huckleberry Finn had the kind of learning we might all envy, school-free and life-taught. Yet for all his disdain of the false values of eddicated folks, he was as busy with self-improvement as the rest of us: he found little to admire in civilization, but plenty to emulate in natural decency and reverence for life.

We can profit by Huck Finn's example. We do not educate ourselves to maintain false values. Nor to be murderers. We educate our capacity to wake to our dream of a world where individuals are free and united. We seem to be always marching through war on our road to peace: at war with ourselves, with society, with our parents, our children, our mates, our neighbors, our ghosts. The old and the new at war within us all. Do we fight it out until one slays the other? Or do we see that peace lies not with a part, but at the center, where the parts fuse to a new form?

At Black Mountain College, the threat of new form so alarmed certain former teachers and creditors that they brought suit against the college, challenging its right to continue. And so the college adjourned, to the liquidation of assets and the paying of debts. In what form will it reconvene?

I experienced at first hand how pedagogy develops in a situation where all concerns are primary. This has been a priceless training for my teaching in other institutions subsequently, where primary concerns tend to be less stressed. And also for my training in community. By living in a situation where customary routines do not prevail, one learns to feel through all routines the personal realities involved. Out of the destruction of mechanical procedure, so to speak, one comes into a new and lively recognition of how forms develop, and one may then act more freely and more consciously with regard to them. By discarding what has become abstract and lifeless, one awakens in oneself a new and joyful and painful contact.

With this hope, one pressed on in the ordeal of one's own education there. Salaries were token, advancement impossible, security poetic. Life was heedless of our capacities to endure its sorrows or its joys, and as certain as our pulse. Individuals who were committed to quality tried to make a life together, where everything was exceptional, an anarchy characterized as much by charity as by dissension. When its spirit withdrew, the college closed. It lives in all of us who there were initiated into a life which has an open end.

The founders had chosen first the name New College. This is significant in the terms I am concerned with: destruction and creation. In order to have a New College, there must be New Persons. Ordeals shall not be avoided. They are the fire. Fear and trembling. The old ego dead, the new man. "Leave all you have and follow me" . . . The frontier lies within.

The figure of Lucifer, the light bringer, reminds us that too much light can blind, as well as too much darkness. We see by an interpenetration of light and dark, and behave by an interaction of conscious and unconscious meanings. Lucifer makes us greedy for information. We must withstand his temptation, obedient to the hand that sows the tree of life beside the tree of knowledge. It is difficult to derive knowledge from life: one has to move gently, observing carefully, lovingly, all the data streaming in. Beware of eliminating data by prior assumptions about what the data will be! We are saved by our mistakes, by surprises, by intrusion, which lead us again into experience and do not limit our knowledge to the edition of our concepts. The cool head is warmed by the heart. The hot heart is tempered by clear thinking. It is part of our pedagogy to teach the operations of thinking, feeling, and willing so that they may be made conscious. For if we do not know the difference between an emotion and a thought, we will know very little about prejudice. If we do not know the difference between a feeling and a will impulse, we will know very little about bullying. We say we want to do away with prejudice and bullying. We need to understand the components at work in them in order to free their hold. A person rarely chooses to be prejudiced; he is driven by feelings which have been absorbed into his organism. This is why it is so important to work curatively through the body as well as through attitudes.

Persons who may be horrified by racial segregation have no qualms about segregation in their private lives on the basis of behavior. The fish all come out of the same kettle: whether we feel superior to a person with a different skin, or with different tastes in art or business, or with different beliefs in politics or religion. The pro-Negro may be anti-Catholic, the pro-Catholic may be anti-homosexual, the pro-homosexual may be anti-bourgeois, the bourgeois apologist may be anti-beatnik, the pro-beatnik is anti-Madison Avenue, the pro-materialist is anti-Semitic, the pro-Semitic is anti-German, and so it goes. Perhaps the segregation pattern is being dissolved from the basest levels of actual enslavement and genocide gradually upward, with the subtler bastions yet to be razed.

What we always come back to is that Pedagogy has as its subject the person. The results of education are character. This is what Huck Finn had. To have character is to be big enough to take life on. If we are able to see what systems we live by, that is a beginning. This is part of the preparation of the clay which precedes the centering. It is hard to do, for many of our values and assumptions are unconsciously held. But anyone can make a beginning in self-study. And the gaps in one's honesty are in a sense bridgeable by the good faith of one's search.

It is hard to let go of those systems. It cannot be done by the will alone and should not be done so. Most of us need teachers. They help us to discover the mesh of spirit which will sheathe our release.

In childhood we can lay the ground for the ordeals of self-examination and transformation that lie ahead. When the child grows to manhood, he should be able to look at himself with candor and mercy. From reverence for life grows a sense of wonder and thanksgiving. The child feels friendly toward nature and himself. He knows that life is full of beauty and pleasure and mystery no matter how muddled it may get, and his sense of importance never deserts him. A certain kind of honor and dignity will preside whatever the circumstances may be. He will be strengthened in his courage to defend life, though tides of destruction may suck at him.

As a child's faculties awaken, they seek the knowledge appropriate to them. An adult needs to be sensitive to these awakenings and not project his hungers precociously into the child. For the child will pick them up instantly as his own. If a child is nourished in a feeling for life which answers the hunger of his age, then when he is a man he may be strong enough to take the powers of his adult hungers upon himself. As we nourish the child's innocence and trust and enthusiasm, we bring simplicity to new birth in our own hearts. His idealism and resistances reverberate in us. To find in the child the seedling of man. As adults, to press forward with the zest and conviction of children, on our way to becoming who we are.

It takes courage to grow up and turn out to be who we are. We face surprises. And disappointments. The crucial fact is that we are different from anybody we know or admire. This is hard to accept in a standardized society like ours, where "character" is a term of abuse. One of my mother's favorite warnings to me was that I should not make myself "conspicuous." It takes all one's courage to be the person one is, fulfilling one's odd and unique possibilities. Though the urge toward conformity may reflect a deeper urge toward union, still local customs do tend to make us dress alike, talk alike, think alike. And indeed we are all members of the same species and there are bound to be basic similarities. Yet in the middle of life we find that we are more than this life has ever taught us. The child presses forward: mischievous, boisterous, shy, tender, observant, mystical. Who is he? The birth of Person is the aim of Pedagogy.

In the alchemist's vessel, the new person was born — the homunculus. Pedagogy, poetry, pottery, or redemptive science are functions of the alchemical spirit. Antonin Artaud, whose warning began this chapter, sought to create an alchemical theatre:

> Where alchemy, through its symbols, is the spiritual Double of an operation which functions only on the level of real matter, the theatre must also be considered as the Double, not of this direct, everyday reality of which it is gradually being reduced to a mere

inert replica — as empty as it is sugar-coated — but of another archetypal and dangerous reality, a reality whose Principles, like dolphins, once they have shown their heads, hurry to dive back into the obscurity of the deep. — *The Theatre and its Double.*

Its power was to be redirective, turning petty sensuality and egotism into metaphysical participation. Ideas of Being and Becoming were to infuse the spectator after a transforming theatrical experience. The director-stagemanager-playwright uses costumes, lighting, objects, sounds, movements, voices, instruments, language, screams, everything he needs to penetrate through the deafness and defenses of his audience. He must reach them. Man must be initiated into the truths of being. He must not be allowed to remain a spiritual weakling and ignoramus. The actor must ACT and the spectator must re-ACT. Themes are mythic. Actors are emotional athletes and virtuosos of movement and voice. Everything is composed to a hair's breadth. Artaud defies anyone who experiences theatre of this kind to leave the hall and thereafter to lend himself to the opiates of war, drugs, and mass attitudes. Our "esprit" may be awakened by a theatre that rouses centers of perception, and once awake, we will not be so likely to drowse into inanity. "Une seule chose est exaltante au monde: le contact avec les puissances de l'esprit." *Only one thing in the world is exalting: contact with powers of the spirit.*

Until we see the relation that exists between our requirements for education and our requirements for theatre, we will have failed in our tasks of centering. Drama originally had a relation to religious mysteries and to initiation of the soul into successive levels of capacity. Artaud wished to renew the "mystery" impact of the drama. Education likewise was originally the work of initiates, who were the teachers of reality. This may sound queer today, so far do we stand from esoteric knowledge. But I see that our education is hollow unless it awaken in us the source, and our theatre is drab unless it kindle in us revelation's holocaust.

Artaud urged his Theatre of Cruelty as an unguarded embrace of reality. "When we speak the word 'life,' it must be understood that we are not referring to life as we know it from its externalities, but to that fragile, unresting center which forms never reach. And if there is still one hellish, truly accursed thing in our times, it is our artistic dallying with forms, instead of being like victims burnt at the stake, signaling through the flames."

In modern psychology, Jung has explored alchemy for its clues to the processes of the psyche:

Although their labours over the retort were a serious effort to elicit the secrets of chemical transformation, it was at the same time — and often in an overwhelming degree — the reflection of a parallel psychic process which could be projected all the more easily into the unknown chemistry of matter since that process is an unconscious phenomenon of nature, just like the mysterious alteration of substance. What the symbolism of alchemy expresses is the whole problem of the evolution of personality . . . the so-called individuation process." — *Psychology and Alchemy*

The importance of the shadow, the dark side of one's personality, in such a process is stressed by Jung, as was the phase of nigredo, the black phase of melancholia in the alchemical process — as cruelty is in Artaud, as destruction is by poets and prophets. The release of dark forces stirs beneficent forces and awakens in us mysterious dawns.

The sense of inner life is common to all. It is this inner life and its intuitions of cosmic origin which stir in the myths and rituals of all religions in history. The religious instinct preserves contact with the powers of the universe and a sense of the destiny of man. This instinct, like others, is often blocked in its expression. As Artaud reminds us, the use of drugs, aphrodisiacs, crime, war, are all detours of the spirit, in a rage to meet life at a level of inflammatory reality.

To live life at the center — to incarnate at the center, so that one's limbs move with that fire; to project ourselves into space: this is theatre, flight, daily deed. We do project ourselves into space, consciously or not. In our Pedagogy we practice an alchemy which draws its fire at that center.

In meditating upon my theme, I have asked myself what I have learned most from, and surprisingly answered, "Poetry and music." Poetry was to be expected, since the world has always shone for me as image of spirit. The earthly miracle is matter. Innerness has seemed less mysterious than embodiment. Poetry less strange and difficult and marvelous than building a bridge or running a business. But music: I am not a musician nor have I studied. The circumstances of life have, it is true, given me intense musical opportunity, as listener. And the listening ear is once again indicated by my answer.

Listening to music teaches through experiences of structure and of tone. These experiences are microcosmic. Structures of music are structures of cosmos and society, and musical range is related to human range. Musical structures, *deeply heard*, develop responsiveness to structures in other kinds of perception. The ability to *hear* the unaccompanied voice or instrument. To *hear* more than one voice at a time; a dialogue between soloist and orchestra, between two soloists, between chorus and chorus, machine and technician. The ability to experience simultaneously variations in speech and tone, as many voices interweave. In music we do not insist that one keep quiet while another speak. Clarity is not linear. We hear that the composition may be made of many sounds and silences, or few, and that what we must listen to is just *that* composition. Alertness for life may be immeasurably sharpened through the ears.

Tone is more difficult to speak about. But I do know that it is a living substance and cannot be mechanically reproduced. Man is a tone-being: *Ton-Mensch.* Listening to tone has shaped my teaching and writing and social behavior. It connects person, organism, spirit center, and living ether. It has influenced my views on communication, films, books, records, television, music, poetry, social action. Perhaps it is the most important single centering force I am conscious of. Remember the potter listening to the rising cylinder.

In nineteenth-century Europe, the musical concept of *Hauptstimme,* or the Main Voice, with accompaniment by an ensemble prevailed. Now there is a move toward Everyman becoming his own Hauptstimme, and the ensemble a group of peers. This is an ancient teaching, the gradual internalization of kingship, the move from external to internal rule. And so in certain recent music, the members of an orchestra are a fellowship of soloist-composers, each choosing, to some degree, what music to make. The spirit of jazz has long had this character. It seems to be a question of tapping the musical center in oneself. And this center will be a function of our total organism. We play what we hear. How well do we hear?

If we can hear, we have a better strength to maintain balance in a world which tempts us into making ignorant choices. The logician tells me that I can't have everything. My ears tell me different.

Well, this has been my education: pitch, duration, timbre, volume; rhythm, harmony, counterpoint; atonality, serial composition, indeterminacy, *musique concrète,* music as happening; ethnic music, nature documentaries — name it. I have a friend who says he has learned most from watching and drawing insects. The stages of their life cycle draw his attention furthest into reality. The egg, the larva, the pupa, the moth; the grub, the wasp; and the bug's skill in perpetuating his species, feeding and building and protecting. I can feel the inner stretch in my friend's dedicated observation.

Study in depth! To press in, extend upward, widen, contract, to develop a feel for the centered position, and then to work out of a variety of impulses. Confirming each new form before we go on. Fingers always ready to release gently. Listen!

To foster a sense of life at its profoundest depth and in its sacred value! Is this not the premise of our Pedagogy?

CHAPTER V

Ordeal by Fire: Evolution of Person

ORDEAL by fire is ordeal by all the holy sparks that multiply, thoughtless of our ability to stand firm. It is Artaud's "cruelty" — relentless. Time is our ordeal, and space. The hot gush. Age; and wandering. The gassy changes. Fire has its slow motion, its flare. Tedium, alarm, necessity. I tell you we are in it. The voice at the center speaks in tongues of flame. Consent. Consent. Its syllables are our tones and clay. It takes a golden ear. The child in man hears his fire rise.

What I have been struggling toward saying through these pages is that perception itself yields moral insight. And centered consciousness yields initiative of will. And thus the ancient Trinity of Truth, Beauty, and Goodness lives in the modern ideal of Surreality, Nakedness, and Freedom. Or Revelation, Redemption, and Compassion.

Le foyer central leads us farther still: *educare*. It is always the prime question: Where is the moral source? How are the laws to be learned in the human will? How may intellect and sanctity marry? Where does one look for the teaching; and once found, how does one use it?

All my life-experiences lead me now to say that life is a script. We may learn to read our deeds and feelings, the heavens and earth, all bodies, the ether and the void, by the fine development of our many senses. What man is, is also in the universe which bore him. His intelligence is part of its intelligence. His organism part of its organism. His sphere within its. As he perceives more and more directly the dialogue of man and cosmos, he sees more than meets his eye. He is so much doing it now. He is involved in his physics and mathematics and astronomy and engineering and biochemistry and archeology and linguistics and medicine with so much that does not meet the eye. More and more the eye becomes an organ seeing into things with more than sight — an organ of contact, like a tongue, tasting; using the energies of imagination and intuition as well as reflected light. In touch, our inner eye stands quick in the membrane of the flesh, and thus we may more wholly see.

Substance itself bears traces of the whole. These traces, as we perceive them (and provided we heed them!), carry us toward the center; they are the paths and structures of our interrelatedness, they are the seeds of our free residence, they may speak to us as Conscience. The dying blooms of divided life cast seeds of awareness. They may grow as the Vine, connecting themselves everywhere. Pure beholding kindles love.

Because the physical world is spiritually formed, the true materialist wakes to Himself. Person is integrated into perception. And the centered consciousness disentangles us from indecision and ambivalence, by lending insight into the nature of what appear to us as alternatives or mutually exclusive opposites. We make our choices in a more peaceful awareness of their relation to wholeness. And likewise, because of this relationship, we have a finer will for exactitude.

Each aspect of human form has its physiology, whether it be the form of the carcass, the forms of the organs, the forms of sensation and emotion, the form of the ego, the psyche, the personality, the form of the future form, the form of moral intuitions. Moral possibilities are carried by life-forms which lead the organism into its future, rather than leave it to perish with its shedding cells. Any seed is so endowed with this life-form that it knows what to become, and this knowing is not conscious. It is a natural intelligence staggering in its consummations.

There is as well the moral form that evolves in man as a species and in the individual, through time. Time is real, things happen in it, and man's history is a story of changes. We don't know them all, but we can observe in the history of philosophy and religion and law and literature — the history of ethical sciences — that there has developed in man a capacity to stand at a distance from his own deeds, to judge himself. Once possessing this power of conscience, he is able to draw from the resources of his being values which differ from unconscious tradition or from the rash utterances of his egotism. We speak in error, we correct ourselves. We act without charity, we ask forgiveness. The moral rule which at specific historical periods was furnished by the authority of ruler or priest or sage, by tribe or clan or family, is evolving into an inner rule, which is free to establish itself because it is just and personal.

I wish to speak very quietly and thoughtfully here; for I am not preparing to tear away any veils. *À cheval sur l'inconnu:* riding horseback on the unknown, that's where we are, but at the same time the feel of our mount gives us a clue to our role in the chase. The surer a feel we have, the less problematic our direction becomes. That's what I mean: the more finely graded our perceptions, the less problematic our responses. And thus do I now understand Plato's saying, over which I puzzled so many years as experience did not seem to bear it out, namely, that to know the Good is to perform the Good. *To know* means *to unite with in the flesh.* Having beheld the world in its ultimate physics, one will have beheld Wisdom. It is by one's warmth that one takes it into oneself. Thus do freedom and obedience marry in love.

Centering in the moral sphere, which is the shape my subject takes finally here, has as its special task the skillful handling of personal likes and dislikes. For in the polarity of sympathy and antipathy is the breeding place of prejudice and indifference. Not to be their slaves is a portal opening. The prophetic artist shall study the laws of polarity and participate in that from which he feels most separated. I am reminded of a sentence near the start of Emerson's essay on Swedenborg: "For other things, I make poetry of them; but the moral sentiment makes poetry of me."

Where art points the way to life, we follow it. Where science informs us of the routes, we are advised. When the innerness of man is energized by the innerness of all the outer worlds, we grow strong in the contact. Thus energized, and graced with vision and alert senses, and equipped with tools, we live forward into "the abyss of the nucleus," as Goethe so exactly put it.

I think it is structural, this necessity of ordeal by fire. The physics of transformation requires it. For structural changes in the moral form of a person are alchemical changes, producing alterations in pulse, breathing, and circulation. They are bodily changes, and nowhere may we experience so absolutely the oneness of the world as in these alterations of body-consciousness wrought permanently by inner growth. Symptoms of growth may look like breakdown or derangement; the more we are allowed by the love of others and by self-understanding to live through our derangement into the new arrangement, the luckier we are. It is unfortunate when our anxiety over what looks like personal confusion or dereliction blinds us to the forces of liberation at work. It takes courage to leave the nest of the tribe or company and the coziness of "we happy few"; sometimes we have the good fortune to be pushed out, or to fall out.

One is brought to a crisis of conscience. The world stands stubbornly before one. It will not yield. I will not yield. It refuses my concern. I will not withdraw. It stands at a distance, I wish to approach.

World, O World! You may be any friend, or society. But dearest of all, you may well be my self. Some blessed adversary within my own nature who sets his jaw against my sweetest dreams. O mine enemy, be thou my friend. He is intelligent and sensitive. His weakness has made him cynical about the possibilities of life. He speaks deeply about the nature of things in order to show how sick we are, and how separated. That he chooses to speak so tells me his true concern. His public conclusions are usually high-minded, though so stated as to be clearly impossible of attainment. When pressed, he will say, "Of course I am humble before the powers of universe and man, I am humble before hope and love and fulfillment, but they are dead to me. I evoke them in a despairing nostalgia, or in a kind of aesthetic trance: my kind of poetry bespeaks the mineral mirror that reflects light. Let me go, for I am lost. I do not want to understand, it is too dangerous. I do not want the fire. Though I am burning in it, I deny it. For I am afraid to think what will become of me. I will be consumed. I will not know myself. All the familiar apparatus of my life, all my supports, will they not be melted away? I cannot risk everything. Only those secret communions at the small flame flickering in the primitive cruse, no one knows of them, those I may permit myself. The secret promenades enraptured. The secret studies. (And prayers.) Ah but if you speak of them openly, I will deny everything." And so does my dear enemy wrestle with his fear and ignorance and sloth, his pride and vanity: And so when I would swoon into his arms with love, he asks me to think twice. He tells me that the world is mad for lack of pleasure, that man has been estranged from joy; and when I turn all pleasure toward him, he withdraws.

133

This is the crisis of conscience to which my adversary brings me. How am I to behave toward his mistrust and pretense? Because our souls speak to each other (for men are surely brothers, whether they will or not), I know what is in him secretly. He has revealed himself to me; I will not betray my understanding of him, although he would wish me to do so. He would wish for death rather than love. That is to say, he would wish to be unconscious in union rather than conscious. To make love in the dark. I ask him to give himself to me naked in the afternoon. He shudders with sarcasm. Yes, yes, I am a whore to him. I do not know how to teach him to love.

(Is this a parable, that half of Day is day and half of it is night? We live our Day's darkness and sleep, and dawn and daylight hours and twilight. Being is aflame, sleeping or waking.) In the darkness of our unconscious meetings, I and my enemy seek one another. In my dreams, from which you notice he does not absent himself, he seems rueful, preoccupied, only partly present: when we make love, he does not take off his clothes and has a bitter and trifling ejaculation. He is in prison. But through the narrow windows of his fortress he can snatch a glimpse of me, and so he makes what embrace he can.

Or he comes in a harsh and massive potency, refusing to be tender, turning away from my kiss. Nowhere wholeness. How hard it is to surrender both body and soul to love. Our work and our play. All our pleasures experienced as the pleasure of love. What could be better than that? To feel in one's work the tender and flushed substance of one's dearest concern. To feel through the minute pulse of one's living that the highest pleasure, in a concrete bodily sense, is the condition of our consciousness. And when I say consciousness, I mean organism. The more fully alive we are, the more fully we live in our bodies, the more fully we extend our energies into the realms available to us as knowledge and perception and feeling and enactment, the more radiant our enjoyment. May we find our natural release . . . it is the dream that reproduces itself continuously in the cells of our bodies, it is the dream that realizes itself in a long series of partial acts, a kind of long poem of life gestures, where part after part stands for the whole. The dream of release works through our play, our sexuality, our imaginative thinking, our artistic inspiration, our "good day's work" mentality; through our interest in drugs, in war, in insanity. The dream of release: to be out of our minds, to be ec-static, to be ego-less, to be far out, to be in orbit, to swing, to be sent; and the greatest subversion of the ordinary dualisms, in the jive vocabulary which says "bad" to mean "good": man, that's bad: meaning, man, that couldn't be better. The fight for freedom goes on. It is built in. We are better than we think. We suppose that because God is dead for us, we are alone. We know ourselves to be ignorant and misinformed and ill-natured: how can we possibly gain our ideals? But the ideal lives within us. We must hold to that mystery as well as to the mystery of our resistance to it.

From the beginning I have believed the world an amazing place, full of marvels, unheard of, not-yet-experienced. In childhood, the future stood before me like a fairy city of splendors and joys: a city with a faintly Oriental architecture, spires and turrets and mosque-like shapes, all rather special in the dream-light of Portland, Oregon, my home town. The prospect of living my life here on this earth of marvels filled me with excitement as well as with shyness, for it was clear that I did not understand what was to be done, in any ordinary sense. The merest banalities fascinated me. I seemed to have been born taking nothing for granted. Family life amazed me. Food amazed me. I tried my mothers' patience by speculating on the origins of certain combinations she would serve us for dinner: as, for example, prune whip. How did anyone ever think to combine the white of an egg and a stewed prune, I mused. To be born, to live with a mother and father and brothers and sister in a house with furniture and appliances and pictures of Byron and Beethoven on the wall, the neighborhood which lay around me, everything shone with improbability and magic. "So this is going to school. So this is growing up. So this is knowledge." Those more experienced than I spoke often of "limits." I mused upon "possibilities."

I was born to be happy, of this I had no doubt. Strangely unawakened to the dark powers, insensitive to evil. I did not come face to face with Fear until I was nearly forty years old. Time and again my life contracted into an agony of cross-purposes, confused aims, frustrated love. What was wrong? Lots of talent. Plenty of wonder and mirth and high spirits. Until even these were quelled. And I entered into the first fire of the first darkness. Seven years later I was brought to another crisis, and I entered into the true fire of the true darkness. Cut adrift, on the great sea of the fruitful mother; from the flock, wandering; my soul restored, more knowingly to flow out of the still waters.

We are brought to a crisis of conscience through our hunger for union.

By our mates ye shall know us. That soul of me that I know in you, not yet discovered, yet to be wooed, won; once possessed as an inner possession, once born within myself through your embrace, then we may turn slack and drop away. The fantasy has incarnated in my flesh. Your doom and mine have married. Oh the mystery of love and mating and friendship is a mystery of the soul. One of the ways I know this is by my dreams. I dream of my friend who carries to me a message from myself. Soul mates, we speak so of each other. Mates within the soul. Is this not the great hook of love? The agony and compelling image of the beloved who bears perhaps no message of any importance to anyone else? Why, why? Why am I under this person's spell? Ah it is my wholeness that I love and here seek.

For the loved one is the adversary. He is the Other. A transformation in the experience of number must take place if we are to be shaped in union. Ordinarily we add one and one and make two. I and thou make two. There are differences between us. How do we reconcile them? We want to love each other and live in peace, but we find vexation and obstacle after obstacle to our free fulfilment. One retreats. The other withdraws. Injured feelings and anxieties prepare the day of separation. How to love? How to create love? How to serve our ideal in daily presence before one another?

Let us now experience number in another way. ONE. One is a sphere; within it, members. In this sense, one equals two. Or three. Or twelve. And so forth. The world is one.

To begin with the whole, and to proceed to the parts. This is a way to experience number and structure and relationship which may help to awaken in us our capacities for love. If I regard my adversary, whether he be my husband or student or friend or child or a stranger in a crowd or an abstraction in a newspaper column, as I do myself — if I experience my adversary not as a second person but as a *first:* if I experience myself and the other as brothers within the same person, within the same oneness of being, this already turns me toward him in fellowship. If I feel myself alone, a number One, and feel him to be alone, another, a number Two; and if I feel that it is my duty to unite with him or to divide the world between us, then I am already full of tension and intention and already the war between us is on. Pursuit and retreat. Compromise. "Understanding." Humbug! We do not need understanding, we do not want understanding, we want to love. Understanding already separates the observer from the observed. It is faintly condescending, faintly superior. All right. It is on the way. We must of course be understanding and sympathetic. But we must be more. We must act in the knowledge of our oneness.

We are brought to a crisis of conscience by our hunger for freedom.

Life wears the look of battle, and sides are ever more clearly drawn. Our lips mutter "peace" while our hands build protective armaments. Our hands prepare banners waving "peace" while our minds take exception to everything. We write "Save Humanity" and contemplate suicide. Somehow we keep to our prayers for salvation, however swamped our natures still may be in self-loathing, loneliness, and brutality. Somehow the ideal survives, if only by rote. We recall the dream and try to bring it to a waking state.

This inner division is indeed a war within man. Or dialogue.

We must, for the sake of our freedom, cultivate a mood sympathetic to natural processes of forming and transforming. Equilibrium in a field of unequal stresses. The balance of a dancer and an acrobat. Or the life cycle of a butterfly. This is the mood of nature: not equal parts of everything, not principles, but uniqueness and fellowship and an ear for both. An ear for law.

When we grasp the concept of metamorphosis in evolving nature and consciousness, when we meditate upon the formingness of life all about us, we can begin to experience in ourselves the stages of our development. We can grasp the fact that at any moment what seems most certain to us is an illusion. It is an illusion in that it precedes and presages a further revelation of ourselves. It is an illusion in that we cling to it and make it a foundation for permanent values, when indeed it is permanent in its meaning but ephemeral in its functioning.

This is the act toward which we prepare ourselves: to incarnate as artistic vision, to integrate, unify, fuse, indwell. So to inhabit ourselves that we may indeed do what we want to do. What a curriculum lies ahead in our New University! How sensitively we may speak to our secret dreams, bidding them forth, however shy and unpracticed, helping them to their feet, learning to roll with the sea, to walk the waves.

Once I had a dream, a short one. I like it because it isn't often that we get a really good look at ourselves in a way that makes us smile, however ruefully. In this dream I am sitting literally on the edge of a chair, talking urgently with someone. I am bending forward, my hands are active. "But we don't know anything about love," I am saying; "if we did, we could teach it."

Well, perhaps we do not know much about love. And surely we cannot as yet put it on the curriculum. Freshman Love, Sophomore Compassion, Junior Moral Imagination, Senior Enlightenment, with Freedom as an elective. With required courses in Second Sight and Speaking With Tongues. And a graduate program leading to a master's degree in Union with Cosmos!

Such a dream haunts us all, to some degree. It is as if a being within us bears images from afar to which we may in our waking work aspire. One of our most excruciating labors is to bring into center the vision and the rebellious flesh. It is a recurring temptation to reject in anger our partial efforts to redeem ourselves. Because the body cannot yet live out the spirit-dream, because incarnation is incomplete — half-man; half-demon, half-angel — one is tempted to judge by action rather than by ideals as well. It is a touchy business. For it is easy to be high-minded. Ready-made goals are cheap. You may easily agree, for example, that centering is necessary and yet be unwilling to bring into center an element of life that does not interest you. It is very difficult to practice what we agree to in theory. And it is very difficult to be modest in our scorn of the gap between what we dream and what we do, and to persevere patiently in our efforts to bridge it. This battle is daily and specific and basic.

Now what is this love? I think it is a spiritual being acting within the person, and through the person. What we call mutual love is the experience of contact between persons when the spirit of love, dwelling in each, moves through the walls of resistance and separation into contact. Like great golden springs which gush into us from some single central source, and which in certain moments spill through us in transformed streams to meet again in a golden circuit.

For part of the mystery is the recognition we feel. It bespeaks an occult saying, that friends and lovers have been companions in ancient corridors of time: we come upon each other suddenly and lo! The unheard-of becomes potential. Possibility becomes power (*potentia* becomes *Kraft*). It is the enchantment of paradise. Rather than the witchcraft of hell. Or the dull suspensions of belief in the inbetween.

At the center, Christ, Atman, I and It.

. . . . the Christ Within : what a beautiful thought!
The warmth and light and love radiating from within,
the fountain, the freshets of spirit-man,
my limbs of the tree of life, my muzzle in the waters of life,
my udder swinging and banging with milk and honey,
and Krishna riding herd on me as I find the holy river of mother earth
and Shiva opens his third eye and Cyclops loses his one,
and one from three leaves two, created by the light of the world
in order that they might see where they was at.

And I John saw the holy city, new Jerusalem, coming
down from God out of heaven, prepared as a bride adorned for
her husband.

The precious stones of her housing.
The mercurial *lapis* in which gold hangs.

The hermaphrodite, the rebis, *artifex* and *soror*, uroboros, the
self-generating impulse
    of which two sexes are our mutation,
and sacrament of marriage,
    the living seed in the magic vessel —
fire in the stone.

Acceptance is part of love. It is devotion to the whole. When the doctrine of acceptance speaks of doing away with the categories of good and evil, it is not in order to turn
everything into good, nor to turn everything into nothing. Rather it is to prepare a meeting
between man and phenomena at a level free of category, of evaluation. This is a preparation for the acceptance of the "is-ness" of each thing. Life then takes on its natural
colors as natural values. We do not create them. Metamorphosis shows itself to us. We
see our abilities transform themselves into each other. Emotions turn into physical symptoms. Bodily rhythm turns into feeling. Powers of growth turn into intellectual aptitude.
Insight turns into countenance. We realize that we are educable. Diet affects inner capacity; meditation affects physical capacity. Everything we are and do becomes a calligraphy of gesture, inner and outer, which more and more we will learn how to read.

    I am brought to a crisis of conscience when the current of love fails (no matter where,
nor how, in whom, nor why the failure) — when separation and, more seriously, estrange-

ment occur, whether in a relationship of personal regard or public encounter. I am brought to a crisis because I am committed to acceptance and to the suffering it entails. I have to accept the separation in order to keep contact with the shape experience is taking: I must keep my clay centered. The natural changes can take place only if I do not stand in the way of the flow of energy. In order to accept mistrust, I have to experience *that* and live into *its* meaning. Acceptance is not a nod of civility, nor is it approval. It is something more like ingestion, a capacity to experience the reality of another not as if it were one's own but indeed as another's, a capacity for self-surrender to the reality of another person (this is a surrender not of the will, but of the perception): honor is a single flame in which all honor burns. The flame of our meeting burns, and in it burn as one warmth my regard for you and my regard for mself. This is a difficult fire to bear, and I feel the strain. It is the strain of bringing together rather than keeping apart. It is the duress of union, of intercourse, rather than the stress of dialectic, of movement and countermovement, stress yielding to stress successively. It is the trouble of stress yielding to stress simultaneously, *orgasm,* a union in which perception and feeling and pulse all pool.

It is this centering which potter performs with clay, poet with music and imagery, person with conscience and consciousness. Forms are given by the mutual yielding of elements to one another. Transformations in pottery, poetry, and the person come about in experiences which center the dualisms, the flying parts, the stragglers. The crisis comes when the elements will not yield. The crisis is to center our obstinacies.

In these moments of crisis, when we are at sea, unwell, discouraged but somehow resolute, I think of what my teacher Francis Edmunds said in a public meeting when he was asked why we who spend our lives teaching the noblest expressions of man's spirit in Literature and Philosophy often show so little nobility in our own behavior. Why does not the wisdom of the texts rub off on the professors? Well, he said, we tend to underestimate our own powerlessness.

In other words, we do not stroll gaily and confidently down life's path, merrily sowing seeds of wisdom and contentment and merrily reaping their harvest. This ecology we are involved in operates by no such simple design. The facts of life are hard. Many forces are at work besides our devotion. A mystery is at work. Forces hinder as well as help. And there is the slow development of man, ages long already, and miles to go before we wake. It helps, I think, to consider ourselves on a very long journey: the main thing is to keep to the path, to endure, to help each other when we stumble or tire, to weep and press on. Perhaps if I had a coat of arms, this would be my motto: Weep and begin again. *Pleurez et recommencez.*

> Tears will make our flesh tender. A soft nest
> for mother-and-child. A soft stone nest for fledgling fire.

The art of non-resistance. One gives up the persona, as Yeats would say, and takes up the mask. That is to say, one becomes that which one is not. Free where one is bound. The physics is clear. The way to center is by abandonment.

And if you are an athlete, if you enjoy exercise and fine coordinations, if you like to stop on a dime from a high acceleration, or go from stillness into a powerful leap, test your limberness and the trueness of your eye, there is no more exhilarating exercise than this "letting go." Practiced instant by instant. Talk about release! One gives in to the outward flow as to a lover. And if one is slapped down, rejected, forbidden to speak, how agile one must be to dodge the blows, how comic and gay the sacrifice of spite and injury, how quiet the union with my enemy.

Am I willing to give up what I have in order to be what I am not yet? Am I willing to let my ideas of myself, of man, be changed? Am I able to follow the spirit of love into the desert? To empty myself even of my concept of emptiness? Love is not an attitude. It is a bodily act. In my crisis of conscience I have to yield myself to the transforming condition of love. It is a frightening and sacred moment. There is no return. One's life is changed forever. It is the fire that gives us our shape.

And yet, though everything is changed, everything remains still to do. Ordeal by Fire is a lengthy labor. But at last we know ourselves under way. And though we may sweat and weep as much as before, we know that the make-believe life is over. We know that we labor upon the true vine that grows in us and that will one day bear its fruit. And as we labor together in this unfathomable vineyard, how fraternally we may cheer each other on in the common task. What could be better than humor and compassion and the savor of life? What could be better than that man's work should become the world's freedom, and man's enjoyment the world's perfecting?

When in the midst of our ordeal, we burn most with resentment and find ourselves ambivalent and faithless toward an unknown and unknowable future, when we are at war with ourselves and others, how do we turn? For turn we must. Conversion of energy. Conversion of man.

I am face to face with the enemy within my own nature, or across the table. *Tout comprendre est tout pardonner.* To understand is to forgive. What does this mean? To forgive is to clear the boards, in feeling. Not to inherit unto the fourth generation the sins of our fathers, nor to perpetuate our own sins in our children. Initiative becomes possible in the moment of forgiveness. Creation may take place in that instant "between."

What is there to understand and why should one forgive? Everyone is in process. We are interpenetrating spheres, we are all centers on each other's periphery. What we do affects the lives of others, whether we wish it so or not. Our physics is subtle and thorough. The sense in which "moral" means something to me is the sense in which religion, science, and art operate out of the same nucleus. The moral value is then compassionate, true, and enacted; a mystery of physical and psychic coordinations is embodied in it.

Since everything is in process and interrelated, everything has its part to play. To understand the meaning of behavior is to envision the process and relationships, to understand the forces that have brought it into being. We will recognize how few of these are conscious. "There are more things in heaven and earth, Horatio, / Than are dreamt of in your philosophy," as Hamlet cautioned his best friend. We are all swimming together, over our depth, groping, trying to find our way, pressing on. Even when the heart has gone out of it, the body presses on. And thus may we forgive.

Who are enemies? Those who oppose each other's will. They do so because their wills are partial. If I give up my will and take another's burden upon myself, we may not be enemies. Together we may make a new whole. It is possible to love our enemies if we understand the meaning of these separations. They are part of a growth which moves toward union. We are experiencing this process when we flow with others toward a center.

Perhaps it is not easy to see separation as a stage in evolution which prepares for union, at a higher level. Nevertheless it is so. The disciplines of centering are meant to help one obey the law of metamorphosis implicit in this process.

All the while I am gripped by crisis, I am changing in the flow of moments. This helps to thicken the plot. For part of the crisis is my ambivalence. Since we live in time, we appear now in an image of despair, now in an image of resolve. In my effort to relate to others, at which point do I fix my meaning? How do I tell the whole story?

It is a function of love to provide a continuous environment in which life is permitted to unfold in its entirety. It informs a moment with the sense of eternity that courses through it: seeing in the child his summer and autumn to come; in the adult, his spring and winter; in the dying day, its full blaze and dawn. It is this Now which holds in layers of transparency the past and future, and we see ourselves suspended in emptiness, an emptiness which exists in order for fullness to be present. I see myself hanging by my knees in my embroidered Mexican work shirt, with no visible support, perhaps therefore weightless, in milky vapors. I look bright and clean and weathered.

Is this not also the potter's chance: to live through, from dust to dust, the life of the pot? Is this what people forget as they look at the glazed vessel, the fired tile, or whatever, what is called "the finished product"? The product is not what binds the artist to his craft. Nor the actor to his theatre. Nor the person to his being. It is the transformations, in their metaphysical vibrancy, and in the life they lead through our senses: the colors of dry and wet clay, the sensations of weight when it is solid and hollow, the long course of the fire, expectations fulfilled and the surprises, imagination already stirring toward the next form, the broken shards, the ground-up slabs.

And is there not a moment when all this stands forth to our perception in any holy crumb?

The pot, the poem, the lesson — the universe speaks in forms that tell us of our own. A vast theatre whose architecture, whose movement and sound, whose episodes have us billed in cosmic roles, speaking lines we cannot memorize for we know them for the first time consciously only when we utter them, developing character and destiny amid what scenery! A symphony of soloists playing simultaneously in a composition the structure of which has been given by the composer, but the music of which, the individual sounds of which, are the choices of each performer. Art creates images of that world that moves within the world. And it is this realm which embodies itself continuously. From day to day in our bodies. From page to page in our writing. From canvas to canvas, stone to stone, dust to dust: the pot returneth.

But there is a difference between a pot and a person. A person has the power to form the dust into a vessel. The clay has the possibility only to be so formed. It is this individual will in the person which can awaken to itself and which can be awakened to what its freedom is.

I have lived my life close to certain impulses in contemporary art. The music of the single sound, the composition of silence, and proliferating galaxies. The poetics of Western Imagism — "no ideas but in things." Garbage art: sculpture out of mashed automobiles; paintings out of old Coke bottles, soiled shirts, window blinds, coat hangers; paintings made out of dirt meant to look like dirt, to consecrate the dirt; an art which consecrates the discard. Cellar doors, walls, sidewalks, street surfaces: as well as all the minutiae of nature. A choreography of making breakfast. Summoning attention, drawing the gaze in, into. And into the wonder comes a kind of high mirth. A release of joy in the form.

And in the "happenings" of contemporary theatre, to what is our attention brought if not to the events on our streets, the happenings of our disjoined promenades, our disjoined conversations as we speak past each other into the next ear. Sequences of dialogue in which everyone speaks at the same time. We chew and chew and talk and talk, and the chance droppings of our talk-feasts harden into the spatial imagery of a poem. Poetry has become a space as well as a time thing. As has music. As has our daily consciousness of dimension: how time changes as we fly through it. Space-time: man's advancing consciousness in the structures of his art. Moving toward theatre, with all the world its stage.

Gertrude Stein helped us in America toward the single word. "Arthur a grammar." The glorious resonance of language: for what we hear with our inner ear is an inner resonance of the being who is named. As she said, making love is saying a name over and over again; nouns carry the grammar of love: a rose is a rose is a rose. It is not statement, it is presence.

There is no longer anything hidden from the imagination. There is nothing mean nor valueless. The sparks lie everywhere within the multitudinous shells.

But I feel there is another step and yet another; this eye that opens upon the rejected may be unopened to other visions. The life that awaits us has no blueprint. It speaks out of all nature and all art, out of language itself, it invites us to live into its mystery, to go with it. It is what happens in my favorite folk tale, the one of the Irish prince who had to go a journey on a little shaggy nag as part of a bargain with some supernatural being. In the horse's ear (note!), he finds a little ball, which he is instructed to throw ahead; it will be his guide. He is to follow the rolling ball, which leads him, as one knows it will, through all the labors of man. And then, when he arrives before the gates of the city which is his destination, he is instructed to kill his horse, his faithful friend who has borne him so surely forward. It is an almost impossible deed, it is surely inhuman, unethical, cruel. Although the command is beyond his comprehending, he obeys. He slays the horse, and from the corpse springs a prince, who had been captive within its form and who is now released by the courageous obedience of the hero. It has been a selfless obedience, for the hero has had to acknowledge a power and wisdom higher than his own thinking. As he gives up his will to it, as he behaves without egotism, nay contrary to what he tells himself is right and loyal, there is liberated a new being, the faithful friend in his radiant form. Is this not a glorious tale?

It is not so easy to yield one's self-will to this higher wisdom. At one level of commitment, we may follow, but with a certain ruefulness, a sense of loss; a kind of stringy petulance hangs from our acts.

We may come to another level. There the ideal *is* the path, and to serve it is to feel oneself expand and lift and sweeten. Now the crisis of conscience brings sweat to our brow, to be sure, but a sweat we sit to with a better patience, a calmer endeavor, a sense not of a moral contract made up of nine parts bootstrap and one part self, but rather a sense of truth which gives us our strength to serve it. This energy mysteriously comes. We have but to breathe. "The soul evolves as the breath penetrates."

But because we aspire, we may not deny the spite that rises in our gorge and over our lips. Life is cruel and unjust. And we withhold ourselves from it for good cause. Why should I care? Ah this is a riddle I ponder on. Why should I care? I do care.

We may not tamper with our anger and our bitterness, for they too move by deeper meanings. This is part of the crisis of conscience. First one clears the air, accepting life with joy in all its forms. Then turbulence rises, and one is angered by rigidity and conceit. One mounts the anger like a vigorous beast and rides it out, letting it take one where it is going. For in the anger lies an angel, a capacity, which can only be brought to birth by an inner marriage, a yielding to it. I will let my anger take me and carry me off. I will awake and the monster will have turned into a friend.

It is important to let the reins hang loose, at the same time to be well enough seated not to fall in the energetic release. To have a good seat, as the phrase goes in horseman-

145

ship; to have a good balance, on center; to ride this energy that strides between our legs and carries us forward.

We sometimes talk and behave as if life were some kind of mailbox, rather than a continuous delivery and reading. All we need is some light to read by. A desire for light, for consciousness, is what is often meant by a desire for communication. Lovers in absence feel each other's presence even as strongly as if their bodies were joined. The union exists. It is anxiety that haunts the mailbox.

In the crisis to which life compels us, we search for the form by which we may best join the world. As we come into touch with other beings, we discover ourselves. This is precise. As I experience the presence of a tree or a field or a stream or another person or a tremor that runs through me with a force of its own, I know myself through that experience. If I turn my glance always inward, I will look into the dark. The dark is real and rich, and it is surely there. But I will know nothing about it by looking into it, for I will see nothing. I will see into the dark only if I look at you. Then the dark will stir, will be stirred by our friction; a light will float like a feather in that dark and my whole being will shake with the creation that then happens.

We are all real. I sit here every morning at my desk, listening to what is not audible, trying to say what is not speakable. Concerned. Connected. The ends of my fingers compose this book as they play the typewriter keys. The piles of cheap yellow paper grow, empty cups accumulate, my cat slips on the manuscript as she jumps onto the littered desk. I cock my ears at the burdock bush outside my window to tune my tone. We must speak to each other in person.

There is a sensology that discovers in man a circle not of five but of twelve senses: touch, life, movement, balance, smell, taste, sight, warmth, hearing, word, thought, and ego. The sense of ego is the highest. It is the sense one has of another: meeting his individuality directly, that here is an I AM as I am. The sense of ego begins to unfold at about two and a half or three years of age, when the child first says "I." It continues to develop if a person allows the child to remain alive in him to the end of his life. Thus in the very sense of self lies the other. Our capacities grow not toward age but toward youth. The paradoxes we find in our thoughts are not paradoxes in life; they are its lawful structure.

One of the parts of a growing tree is the meristem. The meristem is the layer of undifferentiated cells out of which new forms grow. It is potentiality, the capacity for newness, for birth. It is the eternal child. Even at the top of the oldest oak there is the meristem, out of which new leaves push. The child in man.

The forms of life teach us if we but await their meaning. They need us in order to fulfill themselves. They release meaning as valves release steam. The power is not in the valves; the valves translate the power into a language. There is a way of experiencing this power directly, then something remarkable happens. Instead of experiencing attitudes, one experiences experiences. Somehow the mind, as we ordinarily think of it, is gone. The mind is empty. The mind is washed clean, in the blood of the lamb. What does that mean? In the blood of newborn life.

In this blood flow the impulses of science and poetry, life and art, truth as it circulates through us: the dialogue between inner and outer, the centering. There are moments in its pounding when one does not resist the impulse to take people by their lapels and, looking deep into their eyes like the Ancient Mariner holding fast the Wedding Guest, say: LISTEN, IT IS SPEAKING. LISTEN, THERE IS NOTHING TO HEAR.

Illumination grows within us, sometimes like a swift mutation, sometimes like the yellowing aura of spring. But most readily it comes if we give up all that we have in order to be open-souled when it comes. That it may take its shape whole in us.

CHAPTER VI

Recovery of the Child in Manhood

I WILL end this book with my poem of awakening and regeneration. Its composition was a revelation to me of connections I had deeply felt but had not understood. Connections between sea and land and the mind of man. Between childhood and middle age. Between myth and person. Between space and time: how time is curved, how space is made by what fills it. Between alchemy and daily bread.

You will remember that Wallace Stevens said that poetry is a process of the personality of the poet. We may commit ourselves to each other's poems as to a fellowship.

RECOVERY OF THE CHILD IN MANHOOD

. . . pick up the cord
out of the invisible, the visible
out of the dark, the light
out of the heavy, the light :   the seed, the grape
                                    the sand, the vine . . .

In the heavy, hovers the youth's face,
hovering in this face, the child.
Out of the deep sea, the dark horizon, the sun
                              dahlia
                              sun-face, a
falling ball, in time, recovers its fire

to us; the falling man, through time, and loss,
regains;
through all her dying seasons, nature
contracts, by law,
to bear
            seed /
                        as out of absence, the present;

plow / does not make life, only living /
                                    brings to fruit
what ether bore.

As out of the sea, the thing that has been swimming,
as up the dark, the day: the thing
that has been swimming self-propelled
surfaces THERE:
                        prophetic infancy
the man recovers

in this aging face, the child visible: here, just now,
    as we raise our muzzle in the wind to
    sniff
            (and the wind catches a side of your mouth
                and widens your throat and your eyes with breath
                    and you cannot keep your laughter down for bodies don't lie
                        and the solar plexus expanding like the universe and
                            the child riding high, gleeful, until the man shuddering with
                                fear and shame falls over the brink and darkness
                                    films his eyes and his bones shrink back into place),
    as we address ourselves, as
    we point out. As in anxiety,
    our prayer.
            (With our first cry, the doom is set. Doleful,
                we hang back. Aware, grin and gleam, picketing
                    our masters; guffaw and titter, tease the shadows to,
                        come to, and the night will fall as I must fall, and up the night
                            the strong muscle of sleep reaches to starry spheres. There is that

149

                    hope at least, that nature is stronger than our vanity, pull down
                    thy vanity, pull down
                        the set expression, the mineral glint.)
        By the pall-bearers of our eyes, death
        is carried out. Disciples in our eyes unmask. The
        agile tongue,
                        O babyhood!   Flames
in our blood, the shrouding clouds invade, let
the bright spray play, the light strike, the
thunder clap, the weapons of speech sound arms for life un-
drowned, let the bright head move up and the stalk make way,
the mobile bloom climbs all the way,

            your face, grown man, is beautiful
            I can see the child in it
            he is beautiful, he is being born, reborn,
            your face is boyish with the boy in it who lives in it
            this boy leads the way

the man recovers

            flames
            in our veins, run
            their hot red track
    EARTH AIR WATER FIRE
        o alchemy, tricks
                out a man of such sublime
            ingredients,
                    fierce
                        industry, to whet
                                    our
            bursting souls against the bark
                    of time,
                            bring
                in our mortar
                            transformation.

                            150

It is not then, it is not ever,
it is just now, this moment, when

                                the priceless

pearl
        is given.
                 Look in the nacre and behold
the airy figures of what you have been and are yet to be.
Between dark and light the colors come.
Meta-
     morpho-
sis, thin and tensile stuff of worms and
butterflies, plays
            out perpetually
spun, out, pick up the
              spectrum, see the
karma out, I see myself coming to meet me,
hail the phantom with an old hello, it is
my resprouting nature I resow
and harvest and resow,
           my seed I
              bless, pick up
the child
   who wept and leapt and dreamed of levitating worlds, wild
lilies of the field as prime, and elegant, alien and beloved,
exacting prototypes and images of what we are and are yet to be.
O fair fair, the splendor of it, in my mind's eye Horatio,
cruel and rigorous, lit with phosophorescence, an aura of supernatural
release, of all the sensual pleasures and all truths.
O happy fate, I cried, to be born in such a world.
At sunset, I can see it now, an attic window in an American suburb,
yellow frame, over the shingled roof, the opalescent run-off, the
gold and black colossal orbs, day and night, substantial; dreamed then
     grand savages, bare and always full of color,
sinuous, various, single total organism in motion and ensouled,
brought to salvation, saving their

gleaming skins, their enchanted bodies of light,
in light.
How necessary it was in these worlds always to be at one's best:
one's warmest, noblest, most understanding, quietly persevering, healing,
how gracious it was, and perfectly aware of the difficulties and
the earnestness and the perils everywhere, perfectly
aware of how there are no alternatives to love and to danger, they are the
law.
When one grew up, a poet and a missionary, one
would pack the pretty padded box the dress-up clothes were in
with food and gifts and go off to the east, whence
comforts do increase, as the bard says,
(and light does seize my brain with frantic pain, he continues,
when one is a little older). One would go among the heathen,
and have one's energies restored, one's clairvoyance reinstalled,
one's racial childhood reborn — and as new impulses stirred
up one's trunk, in turn one would lay one's hands on those beautiful
strangers and they would be healed by the human touch of personal love
and they would not be afraid to awaken into knowledge as it
unfolds from within, nor to enter into themselves. One would
bring the earth's being alive into their unearthly elements.
One would hazard all one's love in a single throw. Perpetually
hazarded, perpetually replenished. One would be freed by yielding.
One's better self would quest like The Pure Knight for Corbenic,
for talisman, leaving love a foaming wake of
questing. Ha, the myths and fairy tales, how they come alive,
out of childhood, how they come alive now in the man, the
cinders and the peas, the sleeping beauty and the kiss that wakes,
the brutal slaying and the resurrected incandescent prince.
The child saw the burnished columns ablaze,
felt the heat. Stand back! Stand aside!
Let truth be revealed! . . . knew
all the world were members of the flames, signalling, signalling.
What a beautiful perilous physiognomy life has always had, no wonder one
falls in love at first sight.
Reached in her hood of fire,

reached in her nervous system and her bile,
found sound in the lyre her motions made,
felt the image and the tone converge, convert,
felt the language organ grow and jut
between the vision and the ear, a golden walking cane,
a splendid fertile phallus, straightening, straightening.
      Knew as the splendid channel fed,
she was already dying; knew the kingdoms of this world
perpetually expire.
                  The scene unseen: trace
the vine, pick up
                  the thread,
the magic is not in the mirror. Turn.

Ask the question. There is only one.
The king is maimed, and the land lies waste,
in a despairing emaciation of sap, the
vine! the vine!, the spellbound mind
is enslaved by its wounds, the
Pure Knight quests for his king, and he fails,
quest on, quest on,
the perilous rites must be performed.

      Entombed in the shadows, alone
with himself, convulsed
in ordeals of terror and shame, grief-
scourged, aghast, he persists,
battles perdurable foes:

            Penetrates, penetrates
      to the invisible sheath of the source of the life of the light
            of the darkness of the self in the transparent body
                  of warmth and of motion
                        and inner equilibrium self-indwelling, his matter
                        is his home, his heart is his dove, his love
                        is his companion,

his odyssey in time
   returns, Telemachus my son,
   my old nurse knows me by my stains,
   my flaws connect me everywhere,
   I still the wonder on her lips.
   My wife, my son, my dog, all imperilled
in my absence, I reclaim
   against perdurable adversaries.

Earth's fallen kingdom contains its original face.
Genesis peeps
through the orbiting scrawl of nuclear worlds,
seedbeds in their splintering rays,
dazzling playgrounds at the centers of darkness:
the carousel twirls, the calliope twangs,
angelic demons sparkle and brood in spasms of will.
Celestial glimpses
 in the
   infernal force.
The figure persists.

    It reclaims, at the source, the flow.

In the darkness a second birth wakes,
the question rises with mounting energy
out of absence
  speaks the knight, the voyager,
  the wasted realm:
    "KING,
     YOU
     ARE MY BURNING QUESTION.
     YOU
     ARE THE FLAME, YOUR
     SUFFERING
      ENGULFS ME, OUR
     FIRES
      TAKE FIRE."

And the king says, "I am healed."

"King,
   whatever I behold
   is the flame, it
   is the burning question of life and death.
   I enter it, I ask
               the question, I am
  consumed."

And the king says, "You have overcome death."

The metabolism of daily fare turns
   water into blood, bread into body, we
     celebrate communion with
the dead; who are the dead? what is your death? what death lives in you alive
and waits to dwell outstandingly?
                       Initiation is death.
                       Acts decay. Death prospers,
                       nature asks: across the threshold
                       carry the thread.

Carry the throes, sweetest rapture of dearest love
   the blissful pulse of life given to, lover I come and I spend
my passion and my grace in you, life lover no end of spouse
   in the fragile merest giving to. You, of self.

Ho, but the switch of selfhood
   rides a bulging team:
mountainous mind and pitching will and volcanic heart and quaking tissues
— runaways, forging and forming and wrestling with
their fallen chevalier,
   this scarlet lucifer who hides in my branches
and laughs at us with his high white teeth and onyx eyes
and tells us the tale of all the world, his bright brain cocked
and his beguiling face, and the golden apple he holds in his hand
looks good, and we aspire to its polish and its art, it is the abstraction of all

155

the virtues we aspire to, we burn to acquire to, to excel to, and
proudly
        we burn
            in hell,
                  can I pray
to be still
and to wait
and to look
and to listen
and to see clearly
and to take my punishment without flinching

what is peace what is war but the life in our soul?

      Look in the sea, and the wet face of your childhood will be
borne out, moon man.
Water catches light, purples and clears. Color lies
  a radiance
upon the sea, washes out like dye, respires
in the throws of the
tide, the recoils: jockeys
the pale horse from Apollo's stable to the deadly
night shade. Rainbows a London bridge for
child-man.
        Pieces
of eight, the sun
      recovers.
We hold, like grapes,
by the frailest ladder,
our maturity: catch, with our breath, the next new hint
            in the air of the tenderest next step on the ineffable hair
              of the strip we must walk if we dare, the tenderest trip
                from manhood to child,
              the bell in the breast open and clear and
              the softening flesh, stouthearted and lined with the acts

156

that have labored and born, ring through our lives from birth to death
the quest for the child that rises like dawn like leaven like milk
in the bosom that feeds, and we suck on this teat and the
platitudes fade,
the spirit peels its garments away and
stands unconcealed, who is it, who is this man, where do we point,
at what hour do we stand in the
flood and the fire, the burning sand, the kingdom of heaven is now
at hand, the now and forever, you cannot repeal the law of the light,
you cannot withstand the animate hand, you are born and you live
and all beings rejoice
in your perpetual anniversary,
drops of glory
like honey exudes from a bee, drops of love, body's wine, sweet
nectar of union, the fair light heart of the noblest knight
of the realm and his lady, the fairest too, and their child
the man recovers,
all love's children bide and be.

Blessings, athlete
who trounces in the mask of Eros.
Blessings, savior
who launders the trudging soul.
Lips
that press the forward push of breath.
Man
mobile and intact, continuously
shedding himself like old skin,
the bud of himself continuously
pushing out, of his own darkness:

O light's the bunch that clusters there
we tend our fate on a pliant stair
stand supple in the trials of air

We bring to sweetness that child's grace

prepare a place for that true face
fire and flood is that true face

hovering grace in all our manly pain.

The child who wept and who weeps
still
    I take in my arms for its tears are alive
and carry life out my eyes, down my cheeks, down the cracks of the earth
for the yield.

    Keep the waters flowing, Aquarius.
Indwell, Crab. Fertilize, Goat. Inhabit, Fish.
Voyage, Ram. Gore, Bull. Hunt, Lioness. Bear, Virgin, and preside, O
Queen. Weigh, Scales. Embrace, Twins. Be your own man,
Scorpion. Take aim, Archer, and shoot

    a fierce shaft in the quickened blood
    to unite, to unite,
    to enjoy.

        The child
in man
      freshens in
            the shadows.
Dreams hang in
        festive galleries;
imagination turns to deeds the force
that shaped
      our size.
The eye be blank till the stream within
  carry us to our
periphery, and we stand, not eyes,
  but men,

            beholding
what the spirit beholds. Beings be lit
in the ten thousand things.
            Plastic artist,
fashioning himself and his temple, child,
a racer,
            wades like a holy man
into the draughts he drinks,
    entranced, swallows the shimmering view.
    Swells
like bellows the divine exchange,
    a cosmic breathing
between man and all the worlds which he
    inhales.

In the big face of flesh, sits, a sleeping Buddha,
        the child, flashing.
With his beams, blinds
        the organ eye.
        Finds
                his way on.

                        Block Island, July 3, 1959
                        Stony Point, August–September 20, 1960

159

About the Authors

Mary Caroline Richards is a potter, teacher, and poet. She received her doctorate in English from the University of California at Berkeley, and has been a member of the faculty at the universities of California and Chicago, Black Mountain College, and the City College of New York. She is the author also of *The Crossing Point: Selected Talks and Writings* (Wesleyan 1973) and *Toward Wholeness: Rudolf Steiner Education in America* (Wesleyan 1980). Her home is in Kimberton, Pennsylvania.

Matthew Fox, a Dominican priest, is founder and director of The Institute in Culture and Creation-Centered Spirituality in Oakland, California.